Haunted Fairhaven

The Busy Lives of the Active Dead
in the Historic Fairhaven District, Bellingham, Washington

Taimi Dunn Gorman

Manufactured on the Espresso Book Machine
at Village Books in Bellingham, WA, USA

Book & Cover Design by Kathleen Weisel, weiselcreative.com

Library of Congress Cataloging-in-Publications Data
has been applied for.

Library of Congress Control Number: 2012944922

ISBN: 978-0-9860097-2-3

First Published by Chuckanut Editions, Bellingham, WA in 2012.

Cover image:
Wardner's Castle mural by artist Laurie Gospodinovich
(mid 1980s). Photo by James Alfred Young.

Author photo: Mark Turner.

Map: Kathleen Weisel.

Thank you to Bill Gorman for
his endless patience with this project.

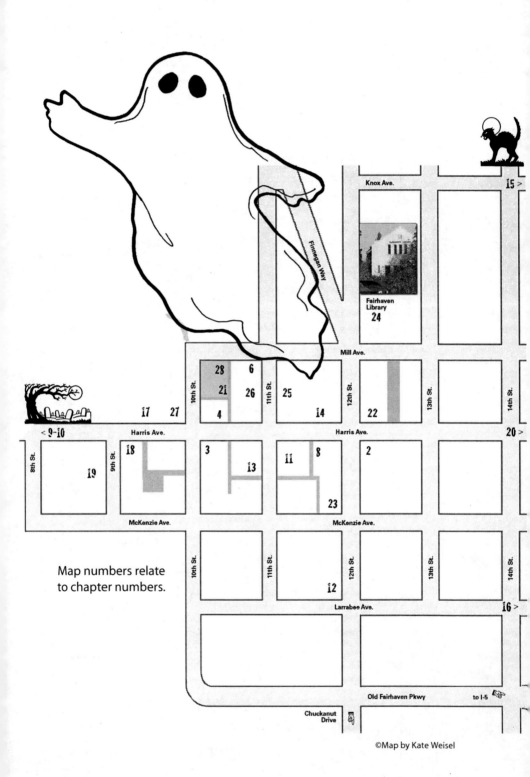

Map numbers relate to chapter numbers.

©Map by Kate Weisel

Contents

Introduction

It was a dark and stormy night. No, really. It was pouring rain, dark and cold. I should have been crawling into bed, but I was on my way to spend hours with a bunch of psychics in yet another 100-year-old haunted brick Fairhaven building talking to and photographing ghosts. My nightlife journey into the supernatural while researching for this book had begun to consume my personal life.

I first became enamored with the spirit-inhabited structures of the Fairhaven Historic District, (a former pioneer town now a part of Bellingham, Washington), in the 1980s, after being asked to write for a group attempting to produce a local "haunted places" television show.

I researched several places, doing a long story on the incredibly spooky Wardner's Castle, on Bellingham's South Hill, and interviewed the owners at that time. Although the show never materialized, my article on "The Castle" was printed in a local magazine.

During this period, I also heard a few rumors of other haunted Fairhaven buildings, but didn't pursue them. I was busy working at our restaurant, The Colophon Café, which opened in 1985 next to Village Books, in the half-deserted 1890's Pythias Building, home of the "secret societies" of Fairhaven.

In 2000, I opened "The Doggie Diner" in the newer Quimby Building on Harris Ave and began experiencing unexplainable noises and activities in that space. I started asking around and found lots of "ghost" stories from business owners and their employees in nearly every old building and even a few of the new ones. I also used stories and references from *The Fairhaven Gazette*, a local history magazine once published by Tyrone and Penny Tillson.

Having collected a group of stories, I published a small brochure called "Haunted Fairhaven" for the local Fairhaven Association, which immediately became popular and was used as a walking tour, especially during Halloween.

In 2012, I was asked by Fairhaven-based Village Books to research the subject more thoroughly, and this book is the result.

In talking to people about their experiences, I found some things commonly associated with ghosts and their interactions with the living. They like to play with electricity, turning on and off lights, TV's and stereos. They can empty batteries in an instant.

They scare people with creaking and thumping sounds, opening and closing doors, turning on faucets, pulling hair. It's hard to say if the spirits intend just to get attention or are trying to make someone leave their space. Most seem benign and some are even protective.

Sometimes they appear as black shadow apparitions, mists or round white, moving or floating orbs that are caught in photographs. Examples of orbs can be found in this book and on www.hauntedfairhaven.com. Full body apparitions are not uncommon and have been seen both in Sycamore Square and Dos Padres Restaurant. Often it's more elusive, like a sudden cold spot, the hair standing up on your neck or a feeling like someone is watching or touching you.

In researching people who had passed away in locations where paranormal activities are found, I discovered a wide range of attitudes ghosts seem to have about the spaces they visit.

Spirits seem to fall into one of several categories. If someone has died suddenly or unexpectedly in an accident or shooting, for instance, they may stay because they either haven't figured out that they should be going now, or they're still angry about their fate. These can be disruptive to the living if they act out.

If a people had a strong attachment to a place, even if they hadn't passed away there, they may return and just hang around. This happens in bars and restaurants sometimes, where they might appear at the same table repeatedly, or in houses they once occupied. They may be welcoming to the living. They may be afraid to move on to the next level. Whatever it is, the Fairhaven Library has a lot of hangers on.

In some cases, it seems spirits stay because they have a strong emotional attachment to a person. The ghost of a dead spouse, child or pet may stay until the living person doesn't need their presence anymore.

In other places, an extreme emotion or activity may repeat itself over and over in a never-ending loop. It's almost as though the energy is embedded in the spot.

"Spirits of both animal and humans, can get stuck on the earthly plain after death", states Intuitive, Joanna Schmidt, L.M.P. "These spirits may have unfinished business, or unhealed anger keeping them here, and some may not know where they are supposed to go once they die, or how to get there. Especially in cases when loved ones are kept alive as long as possible by using unnatural methods such as drugs. When the time comes the deceased may not know where to go or that they have even passed."

I looked into the yellowed 1890's newspapers and historical records about people who had died in less than normal circumstances in and around Fairhaven, to see if I could match any of the current supernatural activities to events from the past. The Washington State Archives in Bellingham was invaluable. I also sought information from Sycamore Square's website, and the website and staff of BOOO (Bellingham Observers of the Odd and Obscure). I read numerous books on the history of Fairhaven, including James Wardner's biography, stories by long time resident George Hunsby, and others. Most of these stories reflect that research. I have attempted to credit my resources throughout and at the end of the book.

We don't really know why spirits do what they do and hang around old buildings. Over the past 150 years there has been a lot of living and dying in the Fairhaven district, especially during the boom years of the 1890s. Some of the more famous deaths included shootings, being run over by a train, being blown up by explosives, or dying in some other violent way or benignly in a doctor's office. There were also the usual human problems, lover's revenge, gambler's rage, robbery, suicides and murder.

Complicating the issue of research is that some people are sensitive to the presence of paranormal activity, while others, not only don't believe in it, they also never see or feel anything in that regard. You may ask ten people in Fairhaven what they've seen and five will say "nothing". The other five will tell you stories that will make your hair stand on end.

My experience is that those who don't believe in things they can't see tend to set up a barrier between themselves and occupants of the "other world". I read somewhere that "ghosts won't waste their time and energy on non-believers".

Bellingham psychic Jill Miller has said that on the other end of the spectrum, some people accidentally "conjure" up spirits because they like the attention it gives them.

I gathered together several people with "sensitive" and psychic abilities to help with research. Ghost hunters, sensitives and psychics, Sherry Mulholland, Brian Lee, Elena Stecca, Chuck Crooks, Pam Castanera, and Tracy Schwent, from "Bellingham Observers of the Odd and Obscure," came with measuring equipment, including recorders for EVPs (Electronic Voice Phenomena) and EMFs (Electro Magnetic Field Detectors). Photographers and intuitives, Linda Sue Hoofnagle and Leslie Smith, captured some astounding pictures. Historian and sensitive Penny Tillson's assistance and photography were invaluable, as was her editing skill. I also appreciated the work of blind sensitive, Kandee Young. Each investigation had a different mix of this group, depending upon who was available on investigation nights, and each person brought different strengths.

I tried not to share specific research with the psychics before visiting a building so there would be no pre-conceived notions. I also interviewed "victims" of hauntings without telling them what I knew until afterward. This way I was able to find real correlations between their stories, with others and the research we'd done.

The names of owners and employees of businesses are real unless noted. Nearly everyone who spoke to us or spent the night with the investigators spoke on record. The stories are real.

Haunted places and spirits can be a pretty morbid subject, but I tried to look at it as objectively as possible. Death is a part of life, but when the dead invade the space of the living, strange things do go on.

Here is a chronicle of interactions with the supernatural in the pioneer town of Fairhaven that thrives into the present day.

An article in the Western Washington University's *Kulshan* magazine quoted me in the late 1990s. "If you work in Fairhaven, you just kind of get used to it," Gorman says. "It comes with any Fairhaven building. You've got your lights, your heat and your ghost."

Wondering if you've got a ghost? Psychic, Sherry Mulholland says any of these can be a symptom of visiting spirits:

- ◉ Names being called out

- ◉ Knocking within a home or room

- ◉ Objects being moved

- ◉ Doors and windows opening or shutting by themselves

- ◉ Unusual odors

- ◉ Feeling touched

To that list I would add a feeling of being watched or a "heaviness" in the room, cold spots in a space, and a sense of sadness even though the place may be light and colorful.

If you have a ghost, it's not always bad, as you'll find in these chapters. We all live with them every day. If it's a disruption to your life, contact a local psychic who can help.

~ Taimi Dunn Gorman

Glossary of Terms

Below are some definitions of the terms used in this book. There are extensive lists on the Internet, including a good one at simplyghost.com.

Anomaly: Something not explainable.

Apparition: The appearance of a ghost or spirit in real life or captured by a camera.

Aura: Energy or life force surrounding living things. Usually seen by psychics.

Channeling: A spirit passing on information through a human, usually a Medium.

Clairvoyance: The ability to see objects or events not perceived through the usual senses.

Cold Spots: Areas of cold in an otherwise warm spot, usually a sign of paranormal activity.

EMF: Electro Magnetic Field (or Frequency), generally higher around electricity, cell phones, and spiritual activity. Sometimes called a K2 Meter.

EMF Meter or Detector: A tool that measures Electromagnetic energy.

Entity: A conscious, interactive ghost.

EVP: Electronic Voice Phenomenon, voices heard on a recording device, generally a digital recorder. Spirit voices tend to be in whispers and cannot be heard with an unamplified ear.

Floating Orb: Spherical image, usually translucent white, though sometimes in color.

Full Body Apparition: The appearance of a nearly complete ghost figure.

Ghost Hunter: Two types—"Scientific Hunter" uses measuring equipment, "Psychic or Intuitive Hunter" relies on psychic impressions or intuition.

Orbs: Translucent spheres of light hovering above ground and darting erratically through the air. Many believe that ghosts prefer to take on an orb shape, as it requires less energy than other apparitions. If moving fast, a trail of light may appear to emanate from the sphere. Generally not seen by the naked eye. Digital cameras capture them best. Since there are many reasonable circumstances (dust, snow, rain, insects, reflection, lens flare, etc.) orbs still remain a highly controversial subject even among ghost hunters.

Ouija Board: Old style means of communicating with spirits not recommended because of the tendency to conjure up unwanted spirits that are hard to get rid of.

Paranormal: Anything out of the range of normality, unexplainable phenomenon.

Portal: A theoretical doorway of energy through which spirits may enter or exit.

Psychic: One who perceives things outside traditional physical laws and perceptions.

Shadow Ghosts, Figures or People: Dark, ghostly apparitions often perceived in peripheral vision, ranging from two to ten feet long. Often experienced small and darting or large and more menacing in humanoid appearance.

Spirit: The actual consciousness or soul of an individual that has passed on and continues to be observed in an area. There are four main reasons that spirits exist: (1) The person does not realize that he or she is dead; (2) there is unfinished business or an unkept promise after death; (3) the spirit is simply saying goodbye to a loved one; and (4) the spirit has returned to offer advice.

Supernatural: Relating to existence outside the natural world often connotes divine or demonic intervention.

Vortex: The center of concentrated spiritual energy usually accompanied by cold spots, electromagnetic disturbances and increased paranormal activity.

Courtesy of George Jartos.

About Fairhaven

Located in south Bellingham along Bellingham Bay, in the northwest corner of Washington State, Fairhaven has become famous for a lot of things including its history and hospitality, locally owned shops and restaurants, century-old brick buildings and ghosts.

The "ghost problem," as some call it, has been going on as far back as the town itself, but has become more acknowledged in recent years through the use of digital cameras and recorders, video cameras, and by visits from numerous psychics to the area.

Although popular television shows now feature psychic phenomenon from all over the world, their episodes usually have significant historical events that triggered them. Fairhaven has had many such events. A lot of living and dying has happened in this tiny area. Intense emotions have occurred here.

Fierce battles for land, economic booms and busts, greed, sin and vice have been a way of life in Historic Fairhaven since the first human stepped onto its shoreline. In fact, it is said that long before white men arrived, area natives were attacked and robbed by northern tribes.

Archeological digs in the now graveled vacant lots near 4th and Harris Avenue have found tools and jewelry dating as far back as 800 B.C. and an era known as the Locarno Beach Phase. Women at this time wore a T-shaped *labert*, inserted into the lower lip for decoration. From the shells around the site, it appears the natives dined on shellfish and possibly only passed through.

An even earlier group lived in Fairhaven at the time of the Mount Mazama eruption, (Crater Lake), over 6700 years ago. So the Fairhaven waterfront attracted the earliest human visitors to the area.

Unfortunately legends abound of tribes attacking each other here. And, as humans are known to do, the violence continued for centuries. When the Spanish arrived in this natural, deep harbor, they built a fort that was burned and the soldiers killed by indigenous peoples. By the time of European sailors of the 1800s, Fairhaven was still a mostly virgin area with natural resources of coal, fish and timber waiting to be taken.

In the mid-1800s, "Dirty" Dan Harris, an American whaler and entrepreneur from the East coast, purchased large plots of land from a couple of early settlers and by 1883 had platted the town of Fairhaven. His later sale of the property made him a rich man and he moved to Los Angeles.

By 1890, with the hope of becoming the Western terminus for the railroad, Fairhaven became the epitome of wild-west lawlessness, with far more saloons and brothels than churches or schools. Part of it had to do with the sudden increase of fortune seeking men. The front page of the December 29th, *Fairhaven Herald* proudly noted that the population on September 1st, 1889, was 180, but it had swelled to 8,000 a mere 18 months later.

"The population of Fairhaven will easily reach 1,500,000 by 1900!" the paper exclaimed.

Shootings and fights, greed and sin, was the way of life for most of the up too 300 men per day who poured into the town to build the infrastructure. There were so many that some slept in tents while awaiting the construction of rooming houses and hotels. Their paychecks were spent freely on booze and women.

Unidentified dead men were displayed at the corner of 10th and Harris Avenues in the hopes that someone would recognize them. They hadn't been in town long enough for anyone to know them.

With so much money around, robberies were common without an adequate police system in place. Vigilantes took the law into their own hands. It was a violent time. Men were shot or beaten and accidents killed many. There was a lot of living and dying going on in a short amount of time. Decent women weren't allowed below 10th street because of the prolific brothels that lined McKenzie Avenue and 9th street.

Local writer, Ella Higginson, described the colorful life of frontier Fairhaven.

"The buildings were painted blue, green, red, yellow. Those of one story only were adorned with high square fronts—to give them a two-story look.

"Every other building contained a saloon, or a variety theater, or both. At noon daily, yellow bandwagons, drawn by yellow horses, went up and down the town. The wagons were trimmed with white; the horses had white mains and tails; the members of the band discoursing enchanting strains wore yellow and white uniforms. Following closely in carriages were the actresses who danced nightly in the variety theaters. They were dressed in yellow gowns trimmed with white fur, their hair was yellow; long white plumes swept from yellow hats down over their shoulders. Violins, accordions and revolvers made original and stirring melody in the saloons from dark to light." (*Fairhaven Gazette*, Winter, 1989)

In 1892, the railroad chose to go to Seattle and Fairhaven went into a depression that wiped out many fortunes and caused many more people to leave. A dozen sturdy brick buildings remained. The people that stayed behind built a town that settled down and merged into the city of Bellingham.

The largest salmon cannery in the world was built on its waterfront. Chinese laborers came seasonally from cities to work the season. The town survived on fishing and lumber mills and the people who lived here were sturdy stock, a no nonsense group who worked hard and built a community that is strong today.

Each decade brought changes. In the 1920s, speakeasies were located in Fairhaven. In World War II, servicemen slept in vacant buildings. By the late 1960s and '70s, a large hippie population established communes and opened their businesses in the old brick buildings. Taverns, artists, and the first espresso shop in town flourished.

Ken Imus, a recently returned Bellingham native, found the buildings in disrepair in the 1970s and began buying and restoring them. His actions, and the historical designation sought by the Old Fairhaven Association, likely saved the district from the modernization fate suffered by most 1890's boomtowns. The historic buildings remained and any new buildings were required to have the look of the old.

Tyrone and Penny Tillson, researched the turn-of-the-century history and kept it alive while the district grew. The link to the past remained vivid because of them and other researchers.

By the 1980s, locally owned retail shops, restaurants and art galleries were filling the spaces. As vacancies decreased, new buildings were constructed in vacant lots where the former wooden structures had fallen. Condos went in, bringing new residents and the Alaska Ferry stopped twice weekly at the new dock at the bottom of Harris Avenue, named for Fairhaven's founder, Dirty Dan Harris.

Despite all of the growth and change, the spirits of those who have passed are still found here, wandering the old brick buildings and playing tricks on the living. Read on to discover how the past interacts with the present in Historic Fairhaven and how the deceased still choose to make it their home.

2

Fairhaven's Spirit Portal

Mason Block, aka The Marketplace or Sycamore Square
1200 Harris Avenue
Built 1890

The Mason Block, 1905. Courtesy of Whatcom Museum.

Full body apparitions, glowing orbs and migrating office furniture are common events at the most imposing of Fairhaven's 1890s buildings, Sycamore Square, originally named The Mason Block, after its namesake, Alan C. Mason. In fact, there is so much supernatural activity in this space, local psychics have a key and use it for training. Nearly every ghost hunting organization in Washington State has visited at some time. There is almost never a time something isn't going on, though the quiet of night brings out the most activity.

Taking up the better part of the corner of Harris Avenue and 12th Street, this massive four-story brick structure was completed in 1890 at a cost of $50,000. The fourth floor was occupied on the west side by The Cascade Club, an exclusive men's organization whose members included the most prominent of Fairhaven's business leaders, and hosted important visitors to the city, including Mark Twain and William Howard Taft. The space is now occupied by a beauty salon and the building's management office next door, both of which report numerous strange goings-on.

The Cascade Club was widely considered one of the finest men's clubs. It was managed by Captain Grahame, who was one of the few survivors of the "Charge of the Light Brigade," a battle between British and Russian forces during the Crimean war. The most prominent and elite gentlemen of Fairhaven society started the club. One hundred men each contributed $100 to pay for $10,000 worth of fine furnishings imported from Chicago. J.F. Wardner, a local investor who built a prominent mansion on the hill, was the first club Secretary. Numerous doctors, dentists, lawyers and other professionals kept their offices on the upper floors of The Mason Block. The street level held shops and the predecessor to the Fairhaven Pharmacy, the Higginson & Hardy Pharmacy, at 1204 Harris Ave. Surgeries were held in the back room. The first tenants in the 1890 City Directory included Fagan's Dry Goods, Hamilton Townsite Co., Great Northern Express Co., and five of the forty real estate offices of Fairhaven. The original painted sign of the Pacific Clothing Company can still be seen on the northeast corner of the building. In the early 1900s that store had been replaced by Wisconsin Groceries.

The first Fairhaven Library was located there before the Carnegie Library was built 2 blocks to the south. For a while, apartments were also located on the 4th floor. Residents included Flora Blakely and the

Marshal Joseph A. Blakely, who owned a quarter of the building, a professional gambler named William Campbell and real estate dealer, S. E. Mullin. Other 4th floor residents included, lawyer, C.C. Holcombe, and Dr. Robert Leitch, MD.

A more infamous lodger was William Absolom Hardy, also known as Billy "Wild Man" Hardy. An Arkansas native, he was co-owner of the pharmacy in the 1880s. His business partner, R.C. Higginson, was more subdued and lived several miles north, thus not forced to answer to some of the excitement Billy stirred up.

Billy had an ongoing feud with an employee of the Great Express Company, located next door, and the two decided to solve it with a fight. A room was obtained in the Mason Block to duel it out and the Marquis of Queensbury rules were read aloud to the cigar-chomping multitude of men jammed around the ring.

The two stripped to the waist and pounded each other so hard that by the 4th round, neither could get off their chairs and the referee declared it a draw. Three weeks later, Billy managed to get into another fight with a passerby on 10th Street. It's not known what happened to him later, but theories abound that his bad attitude occasionally still hangs in the air at Sycamore Square.

In 1897, one Orrin Garland caught his left arm between the sprocket of a slab chain and the chain itself in a sawmill. Despite his pleas to the doctor, the arm was amputated, leaving him no means of employment. Cleverly, he leased 20 of the best rooms of the Mason Block, opening what would be known as the Garland Hotel.

Two years earlier, Mark Twain had enjoyed the hospitality of the Cascade Club after entertaining an audience of 600 area locals at the Lighthouse Theater of New Whatcom in August of 1895. He was lodged at the magnificent Fairhaven Hotel on the corner of Harris Avenue and 12th Street.

Fairhaven was dark and closed at ten o'clock. The group lit candles and groped their way to the Club, (4th floor of what is now Sycamore Square). They sat in leather chairs, amid the mahogany tables, and helped themselves to whisky and cigars, placing money in the IOU box. No servants were there to wait on them. They had let them go in the financial crash.

The men spoke past midnight, with their esteemed guest coughing a great deal despite the hot drink the hosts rustled up. Clemens wrote later of the lack of regular electric lighting in Fairhaven and of the smoke of the Northwest forest fires making things seem even darker. As he told a reporter from the *Blade Newspaper* on August 15th, 1895, "This is the fourth time I have visited the Sound country and have not seen a mountain yet. I am becoming somewhat dubious about there being any."

The inside lobby of the building is wide open, with a view all the way to the ceiling, wood staircases crisscross the East and West sides, offering a full view of each floor and the lobby below. Doors and windows are tall, as was the style in that period of time.

The staircases in Sycamore Square. Photo courtesy of Kate Weisel.

The building has had as many booms and busts as the district itself, becoming a rundown shell by the time it was purchased and restored in 1973 by developer and preservationist, Ken Imus, who, along with son Brad, named it "The Marketplace" and filled it with a variety of small shops and restaurants. In 1995, Patrick Uy purchased the building, making further improvements, renaming it "Sycamore Square". It is now home to retail and restaurants, professionals and offices.

Building manager April McAllister has been at Sycamore Square for 13 years. Not long after beginning work there, she had her first experience with one of the unearthly residents of the building.

While painting a second floor office space one hot summer day, she had the distinct and repeated feeling she was being watched. Turning each time to find no one there, she continued her work until nearly 8:00 p.m. and then moved the ladder to a corner. The space she stepped into felt freezing, as though, she said, "I'd stepped into winter in Alaska."

As she says on the Sycamore Square website:

"I was absolutely certain I was not alone—when out of the corner of my eye, I saw a young woman wearing a long green velvet dress, the type that women wore at the start of the 20th century. Amazed, but not frightened, I turned immediately to see who was there, but the apparition vanished as quickly as it had appeared. Her image however, was extremely vivid, as if it were burned on a photographic plate in the back of my mind."

She claims some skepticism, despite frequent reports by other building tenants about the strange goings on, saying that she can't logically explain any of it. Although she has not been visited again by the full apparition of the "Lady In Green," April says she knows the spirit remains nearby, and tells of a roofer who visiting her 4th floor office (once a part of the Cascade Men's Club), asking about the ghost. She walked him to the stairs as they spoke and when she returned, her office chair had moved from one end of the room to another.

"I guess The Lady wanted to be sure I knew she was still there," jokes April.

Another time she repeatedly heard rustling noises in her boss's office, as though he was working, even though she knew he was out. Three times she went back to look as she was waiting for his return, but the room was empty. The fourth time, frustrated after hearing the noise, she sneaked into the room hoping to scare the ghost away, and shouted "Boo!" Unfortunately, her boss had just gotten back and it scared them both.

A not-so-funny incident took place when a late-night drinker from The Black Cat Restaurant on the third floor fell asleep on a bench in the open lobby on the first floor. Unnoticed by the staff, he was locked in and awoke in the middle of the night to find everyone had left.

Since it wasn't long until morning, he decided to await someone open-ing the building, and sat in a chair at one of Mambo Italiano's restaurant tables. The chair opposite him suddenly pulled itself out, and then pushed back to the table. In a panic, he rose quickly preparing to throw a chair through the glass to escape. Something seemed to stop him. Thinking better of it, he pulled the fire alarm. When he explained about the ghost, the police didn't press charges.

Mambo Italiano staff have reported seeing a man with a beard dressed in period clothing, standing behind the bar at closing. If approached, he disappears. In 1903, the Unique Theater show house occupied that space, charging ten cents admission. Perhaps it's the doorman. Workers at The Black Cat have often talked of apparitions sitting at tables.

Psychics and ghost hunters from BOOO (Bellingham Observers of the Odd and Obscure) have visited Sycamore Square numerous times, communicating with the active ghosts and often capturing electric voice phenomenon (EVP). Between their conversations with the entities and research on the building's residents, a few things have been speculated about their identities.

In March, of 1892, Flora Blakely, wife of town marshal, Joseph A. Blakely, died suddenly.

A newspaper article at the time said:

"Flora A. Blakely, wife of City Marshal J. A. Blakely died on Tuesday evening after a brief illness. Her death was unexpected and was a sorrow-ful surprise to many friends. The remains accompanied by Mr. Blakely and his little son Roy, were taken to Brownsville, Oregon, for internment on Thursday afternoon. Funeral services were conducted by Rev. J. C. Wright."

The newspaper didn't report the cause of death, but it may have been during childbirth, common at the time. However, another, more sinister theory repeated by visiting psychics is that she fell from the fourth floor. Either way, the couple lived in the fourth floor corner apartment, (to the far right as you get off the modern elevator). Reported often by psychics from BOOO, is that the energy outside that office feels as though your feet are sinking into the rug.

Flora's funeral was held in the lobby before she was taken to the family plot in Oregon. Flora and Joseph now seem to make themselves known fairly often and mediums have reported her leaning over the bannisters or moving down the stairs, while he stands on the fourth floor watching people come up the stairs.

Rich Rowland, who was investigating the building with BOOO one night captured a photograph of a black figure standing on the mezzanine. It may be viewed on www.hauntedfairhaven.com.

For the first three years of investigating, BOOO visitors heard only male voices until they brought a dog along on a visit. The Rottweiler was terrified of the 4th floor, not wanting to go up. He was so nervous he pooped on the 3rd floor landing. Psychic, Sherry Mulholland took him out for a walk, feeling a strong sense of anger coming from the building.

Brian Lee, who often sees the departed, then recorded an EVP of a female voice saying, "It's about the dog." It seems Flora had finally said something. Back in the lobby, the dog put his head in Sherry's lap, while an apparently annoyed Flora would not communicate any more that night.

After that, women came to speak more often. Ghost hunter, Kathleen, recorded a female voice saying "Hah, Kathleen." The voice is clear and affectionate. A young college student, who joined BOOO for a few months, was by herself on the 4th floor across from Flora's apartment asking for something to speak into her recorder. Remarkably, she recorded a male and a female voice simultaneously and softly saying "yes."

Psychic, Pam Castanera says that Marshal Blakely got very close to her during a visit one night in the building.

"I felt the warmest, most loving energy and my EMF went off, beeping like crazy. I couldn't see anything but silver and gold sparks of shooting light and my ears were buzzing with white noise. It was as though I was in this loving, insulated bubble for at least five minutes."

From the BOOO website, it is reported that a woman in a risqué red dress, who calls herself Isabel, likes to entertain paranormal teams, and may have been a lady of the evening. A robust and affluent appearing gentleman in a three-piece wool suit, calls himself Jonathan and may have been a member of the Cascade Club. It's reported he likes to hang out at The Black Cat restaurant on the third floor.

Sycamore Square tenants on the 2nd floor tend to report doors rattling, while others find their chairs turned in the morning as though looking out over the sunset on the bay the night before. One office reported an unplugged printer putting out blank pages overnight.

Local artist, Richard Bulman, who worked at a first floor art gallery on the Harris Avenue side in the late 1990s and early 2000s, felt accompanied by a female energy when he walked up and down the stairs. He reported that it seemed, "always there and just out of the corner of my eye." He felt the energy of the building seemed sometimes "sad." Dogs visiting the gallery with their owners would inexplicably all walk to the southwest corner of the gallery and bark at nothing.

Psychic Brian Lee reported separately, that he'd had his electromagnetic frequency meter (used for ghost hunting) go on and off suddenly fairly often, "as though Flora were rushing by me on the stairs."

In another strange dog-related story, building manager, April McAllister took a series of four photographs of the figurines of a man and woman in 1890's garb on the wall at the entrance to the building on the Harris Avenue side. When uploaded, the third photograph was not the artwork at all, but a picture of a dog with a blurred background.

"There was no way that picture could have appeared inserted between the 2nd and 4th photographs that day," says April. "It's a mystery to me."

Numerous visitors to the building at night talk of sounds of a raucous party going on. From the lobby, it sounds as though it comes from the 4th floor, but from the upper floors, it seems to come from the lobby. April says "the party seems to be in another dimension, leaking through."

BOOO has recorded no less than a dozen Class A (very clear with intent) EVPs (Electronic Voice Phenomenon) in the building, many of which seem to be raucous and sometimes profane. Sherry Mulholland spent one morning playing them for me. Some contain creepy laughter, a woman screaming, or moaning, often while the ghost hunters are talking to each other about something, unaware of the background sounds.

One particularly clear recording happened in the early morning hours as the group sat at the Mambo Italiano Restaurant tables in the lobby talking about the evening. A clear, booming voice was recorded of an African American male with a southern accent saying, "A real gold coin," followed by a slap on the table as though he were placing a bet.

More modern voices have used slang, like "Yeh, he's a weirdo," and "Like, what's up, bug off." One gravelly man's voice sounds like Clint

Eastwood saying "Is this music going to be on all night?" A particularly grumpy male growled, "Get outta here." I've posted some of these EVPs on the website www.hauntedfairhaven.com.

Since none of the BOOO investigators carry recorders that play back out loud as things are recorded, they generally don't know until after they've left that they picked up something. Some are responses to what is going on, while others are unrelated.

It's hard to say why the large variety of spirits visit Sycamore Square. Except for the Blakelys and a couple others, most are recorded just once, as though they were passing through.

Mulholland has a theory that there may be a portal in the building, saying that sometimes water features, like the fountain in the lobby, can initiate energy. Because of the history of places like the Cascade Gentleman's Club, which was likely a place for drinking and fun, all the way to the present day popular bar of The Black Cat, a party atmosphere pervades most of the time. One spirit told the psychics that he likes to enter the bodies of drinkers in the bar, to feel inebriated.

During WWII, the building was filled with soldiers, as was the majestic Fairhaven Hotel, right across the street. By the 1960s, hippies coming to Fairhaven, also known as "San Francisco north," likely used it as a flophouse. When purchased by Ken Imus in the 1970s, his son Brad reports that it had mattresses in every room. They cleaned and restored the building, stopped the leaks in the roof and rented out the spaces to local artists, restaurants and businesses.

Known first as La Creperie, then Le Chat Noir, The Black Cat Restaurant was famous for its European atmosphere, with tables along the railings of the 3rd floor. Their tea, brown bread and crepes were popular.

Local artist, Laurie Gospodinovich painted a haunting mural in the back room of the restaurant. The room fell victim to arson and burned in 1984. The restaurant was a favorite of hers. She had earlier painted an enormous 3-wall mural at Wardner's Castle (see chapter on Wardner's Castle). Gospodinovich died on August, 22nd, 1984, at the age of 21 in a motorcycle accident. It is said she still visits the restaurant.

Joanna Schmidt, L.M.P, a psychic and massage therapist, recently moved her office onto Sycamore Square's 2nd floor. I asked if she had experienced anything unusual in the building.

"When I moved in, I did a 'space opening,' respecting and acknowledging who was there, and explaining my intentions," she said. "I asked that I be left alone to do my work."

Schmidt also said that she talked to "the building as an entity" asking permission to be in that space and she promised to "be good to the building, leaving it in better shape when I leave, than when I came."

She got a reminder of that promise one day while in a rush she flew into the bathroom stall, accidentally banging the door against the tile. As she felt bad, the lights blinked a couple of times.

Now, with modern businesses and health care professionals, a fashionable shoe store, cigar shop, professional offices and two restaurants, the Mason Block is still a dominating place in Fairhaven, and it appears, one of the most haunted, too.

3

Orbs, Artists and the Unknown Dead

The Morgan Block
1000 Harris Ave
Built 1889

Now an artist-owned co-op building, the Morgan Block is home to painters, jewelry designers, woodworkers, potters and, well, ghosts. Between the hard driving energy of the now long gone saloons and the brothel that came to occupy the upper levels in its years of decay and neglect, spirits have taken up residence and aren't leaving any time soon.

Phillip and Mary Ann Morgan constructed The Morgan Block in 1889 to satisfy the desperate need for more saloons and hotels during Fairhaven's boom years. A wood building with brick veneer facing Harris Avenue and 10th Street, The Morgan House Bar occupied the corner ground floor with the hotel up above.

In 1890, one of the residents of the hotel, Dr. McKinnon, saw patients there, including fellow boarder Charley Swain, who was shot in the knee cap while drinking at the Beer Garden of the nearby brewery on what is know Fairhaven Parkway. Carried back to his room in a cart, the doctor performed the amputation in his room. (*Fairhaven Gazette*, Summer, 1996)

Morgan House. In the 1890s the building had the dubious honor of sitting beside the viewing area for the "Unclaimed Dead". During the 1890s and 1900s thousands of transients came to build the "New City of Fairhaven." Some died of exposure, accidents or suicide. When such men could not be identified, they were loaded into a wagon and put on display in hopes that someone would recognize them.

Marker created with city grant monies and Old Fairhaven Association donations to note viewing place for unidentified dead, (historical markers located throughout the district were researched and grant application made by historian, Tyrone Tillson). Photo by Taimi Dunn Gorman.

Due to the large number of new strangers arriving daily, if an accident happened, or bodies were found, and no one claimed them, they were likely interred at Dead Man's Point at the foot of Harris Avenue. Marine Park now sits on some of the cemetery land, which has been leveled and graves removed.

A 1901 *Reveille* reported that, "J.G. Bollong, a merchant of Fairhaven, found the body of an unknown man yesterday afternoon.... The case was pronounced a suicide. A stick of dynamite and some caps were found which made it certain that the chest of the deceased had been blown out with this powerful explosive. The body was exposed to view at the corner of Harris Avenue and Tenth Street for identification, and hundreds of people, including a large number of the mill men, coming up from their work, viewed the remains, but no one seemed able to identify them." (*Fairhaven Gazette*, 1993)

By 1904 the Baltimore Oyster House was run next door as a saloon by Swedish Immigrants, Louis and Hilda Swanson, along with sons, Charles and Edward. The family purchased the Morgan Block in 1900. After the 1910 ban on alcohol, the Oyster House became a billiards parlor and restaurant.

Baltimore Oyster House, 1905, courtesy Whatcom Museum. To the right of the photo is the stairway entrance to the Morgan Hotel.

The upstairs rooms continued to be run as a hotel, and reportedly, later, an active brothel, fueled by the busy saloons downstairs. It was reported the saloon gained a bit of notoriety when one patron was shot twice through the stomach and once through the heart. The coroner naturally concluded that he had committed suicide. (*Fairhaven Gazette*, Summer, 1986)

Through the decades of Fairhaven's depression, years of decay followed for the poor Morgan Block, until it was finally purchased in the early 1970s as a cooperative for artists, and completely renovated. Now it is home to a woodworking gallery and a pottery shop on the main level, with numerous local artist studios upstairs where hotel rooms once were. Having heard a few stories of activity, doors opening and closing by themselves, and radios turning on and off, I brought in several psychics and two photographers in March of 2012.

The First Investigation

We gathered at 5:30 p.m. and found the door on Harris Avenue to the stairway locked, which was odd because I had just seen one of the artists go in. I knocked a few times and three surprised artists came downstairs and told us they had all left it unlocked for our visit. The door had locked itself while they stood at the top of the stairs talking about us arriving late.

With the shops on either side of the main floor, the center door goes directly to a steep wooden stairwell to the second floor and third floors. No one can arrive or leave without walking those long stairs, or going out the back fire escape. The lock must be turned and it cannot lock automatically. We sensed right away that something or someone wasn't happy about our visit. We hauled our equipment up the long stairway to the third floor for a meeting and to split up for the investigation.

Artist Ben Mann's studio is full of his colorful pictures and occupies what was at one time, a double hotel suite. He does business and computer work in one room and paints in the other.

The psychics felt the presence of a large, scruffy man who called himself "Walter," and the scent of body odor, garlic, and wood chips surrounded him. He seemed to be a "logger type," a kind of guy who would have been very common in that 1890's era. After awhile, they sensed a young woman in a white dress enter the room looking for something.

Ben showed us an extremely old black and white headshot picture of tired-looking woman in black. He had found the picture in the wall when repairing the plaster. She looked sad, but because of the slow shutter speed, people didn't smile in pictures back then. It was taken at the photo studio of R.S. Campbell in Norfolk, Virginia. We asked the spirits who she was with no success.

It was a noisy evening. Being daylight savings time, it was still light outside and people were walking on the sidewalk below talking, with children playing. Our EVP recorders picked up only ambient noise and a few thumps that sounded like footsteps, but it was hard to tell.

We asked Ben if he had strange experiences in his cheery space and he told us bluntly that he had spent two nights sleeping there and would not do it again.

"It was not comfortable," he said. "It was as though I was not alone."

Often while painting, he feels as though something is watching him, but it doesn't seem malevolent and doesn't hinder the creation of the popular folk/café art he sells.

In the second studio on the 3rd floor, Nancy Canyon creates large, soothing floral paintings. Our EMF picked up energy and went to orange and red when I asked about the sage Nancy kept on a shelf. Sage is often burned to dispel spirits and clear the space. A female energy seemed present and the group perceived pain on the left side of her face and foot, and nausea as though she'd been beaten or hurt.

We decided to leave only 3 people in the room to make contact, and when psychic Brian asked if he should leave, the meter spiked to red. He came out into the hall with the rest of us. The two women who stayed tried to make contact, but were unsuccessful, sensing nothing but the fragrance of lilies.

At last, we got a measurable result of activity. A large, bright floating orb with a yellow rim appeared in a photograph I took in the third studio, where Marijo Martini crafts jewelry. She had asked us to visit because her radio kept turning itself on and one day she came in to find the French Canadian station playing fairly loudly. She had never heard the station before and none of her stations were preset on the buttons. Something had specifically chosen that channel. A light perfume scent was in the room that Marijo did not recognize, and none of us were wearing fragrance.

As we ended, we noted that "Walter" and the perfumed woman didn't seem to appear together at any time. Perhaps they were avoiding each other. After a little over two hours, we called it a night.

I was disappointed in the lack of evidence for the night. It had just been too noisy both inside and out. Three weeks later we decided to go back in with a smaller team of two psychics, a photographer and myself.

The Second Investigation

Two of my team were running late, and since they were new to the building, I sat at the top of the long staircase waiting their arrival. The wood stairs, floors and walls still reveal years of use. Although the building has been kept up, it remains very much as it looked when the ladies of the evening led their customers up those steps to the promised paradise that waited on the upper floors.

I began randomly shooting pictures on my small camera from the top of the stairs. Then Leslie, the professional photographer showed up, and I tucked it away and we went upstairs. At the end of the evening, Leslie had shot two good orb photographs, one of them floating in the skylight on the top floor. An EVP recording of a voice answered our question "are you the beautiful woman in the white dress?" An answer came from a female, "Who is that?"

When I got home, I uploaded my pictures. There were a number of shots of the old hotel doors with their transom windows above and several pictures I took of the long staircase down to the front door. Floating in the center of one picture above the steps was the same orb with the yellow edge that I had photographed last time. But there were more. I blew up the picture and tried to count the white circles. There were at least seven. They appeared in no other photographs I took.

Staring at it later, I felt the strong sense that they had gathered to look at me. I was exhilarated and afraid all at once. Ghost hunting was getting personal. I had a feeling much more was yet to come in these investigations.

Cropped photograph of orbs above Morgan Block Staircase.
The one in the center has a yellow rim. There were numerous,
fainter orbs to the left before cropping.
(More pictures at www.hauntedfairhaven.com).
Photo by Taimi Dunn Gorman.

4

Harris Avenue Haunts

The Quimby Building
1001 – 1007 Harris Avenue
Built 1992

On the north side of Harris Avenue between 10th and 11th Streets is a newer structure built by the Imus family, known as the Quimby Building. In the late 1800s and early 1900s a string of businesses thrived at 1001 to 1007 Harris Avenue, leaving behind a supernatural imprint that haunts the current tenants.

In 1905, professional photographs were taken of nearly every business in town to feature in a national exhibition, showing off how modern the city had become. At that time the Capitol Bar held a non-stop party at 1001 Harris Ave, while a cigar shop and a "tonsorial parlor" with baths rounded out the block.

One hundred years later, in 2000, I opened a pet boutique and café known as The Doggie Diner, in the spot where the tonsorial parlor once tended to men's personal needs at 1007 Harris. The strange events there inspired me to write a brochure on Haunted Fairhaven, which has morphed into this book. Below is a chronicle of my experiences there.

IT was there again. Working in the mezzanine office above my store, I could feel its presence in the room. It wasn't especially threatening, just

a strong energy observing me, standing behind me
enough to breath on me. As always, I was extre
a strong urge to leave. Needing to stay and work

“Everything’s OK here,” I pleaded. “You can go
leave.”

I went back to typing. It seemed to be gone, or perhaps I just wa
thinking about IT anymore.

The Doggie Diner served food to people and their dogs. The people food was delivered from The Colophon Café, my restaurant next door, packed as takeout. The dogs dined sitting on bar stools, eating off of colorful Fiestaware dishes, the people ate from paper plates. We also sold toys, treats and clothing for dogs, along with stuffed animals, statues and things printed with dog images that people like to collect or give as gifts.

It was very popular and became a media sensation for the novelty of dogs dining with people. Within six months there were articles in *Good Housekeeping, People Magazine, Reader’s Digest* and the British, *Hello*, to name just a few. TV cameras and reporters crowded the shop some days so that people could scarcely pay their bill.

Between the chaos was quiet time in the store. Before we opened and in the evening the strangest things would happen.

Several businesses had occupied the space at the new Quimby Building before us, none of them staying a very long time. They included an interior decorator, an art gallery and a couple of restaurants.

Long before this building had been built in the 1990s, there had been other occupants of a wooden structure dating to the building boom in Fairhaven in the 1890s.

There aren’t a lot of records of the businesses occupying the space, except for Benton’s Bath Parlor and Tonsorial Palace. In 1889 The Capital Bar was where Bead Bazaar now sits. Going up the block to the East was McCarty’s Lodging House, Mc’s Restaurant, a cigar factory and the Blue Front drug store.

At any rate, the energy that remained behind on that spot seemed to seep into the year 2001 at The Doggie Diner.

The first incident happened as our tall, blonde manager, Sandy, (name changed) was preparing the store for opening. There was a tug on her ponytail and a voice clearly said “Good morning, Sandy.”

Capitol Saloon. Courtesy of Whatcom Museum.

She turned, expecting to see one of the other employees, but no one was there. As a Christian who did not believe in ghosts, this was startling for her.

Other things began to happen. A clock flew off a wall and hit an employee's boyfriend on the head. Noises came from the upstairs office whenever I left for the day. A chair rolled around and there was typing on the computer.

And then, there was the mysterious sound of babies crying when no one was around. One morning I came in to find an entire display on a glass shelf had crashed to the ground.

By this time the staff was freaking out. I often came in to find that the night closer had called a friend or the restaurant next door to have someone sit with them for the rest of their shift. The energy that was present in my office during the day increased at night, and I felt so much discomfort, I avoided going there after dark even though it was my own shop.

My business partner from the Colophon Cafe played jokes on me, moving our sage bundle (burning sage is often used to scare spooks) around the office or rearranging papers, but no one could explain the other incidents.

Once I left my office for a few minutes and came back to find some-one had repeatedly typed LLLLL on an entire line of the computer, as though they had just left their finger on the key. No one had been up there but me.

It wasn't the ghostly occurrences that made me put the business up for sale, but the exhaustion I felt from running the place while trying to keep up with what went on at my other restaurant, The Colophon Cafe. I decided I wanted to visit The Doggie Diner, not own it.

I called a real estate agent friend to list the business for sale. As she wrote it up I told her about the "ghost". She stared.

"You have to put that in the listing," she said firmly.

"You're kidding!" I replied.

"No, it's the law now that if there are ghosts, or even if someone died on the property, you're supposed to say so," she explained. "Someone could come back later and say you didn't tell them and sue you."

So, the listing was drawn up with the ghost included. Within a month a woman offered cash for the Doggie Diner, now very famous and doing consistently well in sales.

In our first conversation I mentioned the ghost. She was unabashed.

"I have one at home," she said. "I don't mind."

Her history with the Doggie Diner was brief, however. Six months after she bought it she went out of business.

Since then, I occasionally ask the current tenants if anything strange ever happens. Waiters at the Italian restaurant that followed, mentioned tray stands falling for no reason and the occasional glass shattering, always in the area where my office had been.

In 2012, it was over ten years since I left my shop and there was now a Mexican restaurant in the space. Out of curiosity, I invited two psychics Pam Castanera and Brian Lee for a margarita in the upstairs bar at the table in the space where my desk used to sit.

Pam set an EMF (Electro Magnetic Frequency) detector on the table. These little devices have an arrow that goes from green to yellow to red when the electrical impulses are strong in the area. Some things that can make it move are cell phones and other electronic devices, but it also tells you if spirit energy is nearby. Brian looked around to be sure there was nothing that would cause interference. We ordered our drinks and began talking about my ghost experiences in the space.

The meter began to move and flashed from yellow to red. Brian looked at the table beside us and told us there was a man in old-fashioned clothing sitting there. He drew a picture of a man in a wool suit.

"He either has a lot of hair or is wearing a hat," said Brian. "He looks like he's wearing 1960's clothing."

Pam and I looked at each other. He had brass buttons, high boots, a watch chain and a long handlebar mustache. This was not 1960's clothing, it was an 1860's uniform!

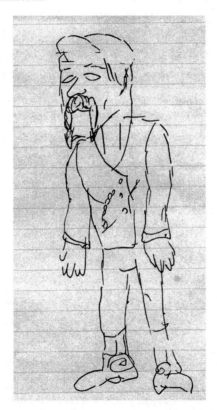

Drawing of spirit by psychic Brian Lee at 1007 Harris Avenue.

"He was in the restroom with me earlier, staring into the mirror," said Brian matter-of-factly. "He was grooming his mustache."

I asked the invisible entity if he was here at the barbershop. The meter fluctuated to red in response. I asked if he had been bothering me at the Doggie Diner. The meter stayed green. Eventually, we finished our drinks and left. My first experience with the psychics had been educational.

As I did more research for the book I found a picture of the Fairhaven chapter of Civil War Veterans in an old *Fairhaven Gazette*. Historian Gordy Tweit had the original photograph. I tracked it down in his archives. The soldier in the center has a resemblance to the drawing Brian created. It appears the Fairhaven Civil War Veterans are still visiting Benton's Tonsorial Parlor for a shave and a haircut.

Fairhaven Chapter of Civil War Veterans.
Photo courtesy of Gordy Tweit.

Psychic, Sherry Mulholland said that although most people look to old buildings for psychic activity, newer buildings can contain paranormal activity as a remnant of what was there before. She said she had previously visited 1005 Harris at the invitation of a former antique shop owner in the space next door to the Doggie Diner.

"One of the most bizarre phenomenon is the appearance of dimes out of nowhere that end up on the counters, as if to seek the attention of the shop's clerks and owners," she wrote.

I knew of that story, as I had also been in there one day shopping and the owner showed me a dime that she would hide around the store and it always ended up back on the counter, as though a child were playing tricks.

Mulholland went on to tell something even stranger.

"It was a beautiful spring afternoon with customers looking at merchandise while others were cashing out at the register. We were standing in front of the glass and metal door getting ready to make our leave after our discussion with the store's owner, when the door opened widely as if someone was entering but clearly no one was there. And then as if to have already entered, the door shut.

My two companions were happily surprised to be witness to the shop's strange occurrences. Whoever opened and closed the door was not visible to any of us. I only wish I had my video cam with me at the time.

Spirits have proven to be such show-offs when you're not filming. Take levitations for instance. Fragile objects lifted and lowered to their original position, so it appears they don't want to do damage, but just want everyone present to know they are there. Or possibly just to show they can do it."

When investigating the building with psychics, she found child spirits playing hide and seek, calling out to each other. While we may never know why they are there, it may be noted that cigar shops often hired children.

The shops and restaurants in the Quimby Building seem to still be home to those who came before, playing tricks, scaring people and moving items around. I wasn't the first to be plagued and I'm sure I won't be the last.

5

About Orbs

When I first began writing this book and doing ghost-hunting investigations, I found that transparent white "orbs" were appearing frequently in my photographs. I had never seen them before. When I was told what they were, I emailed my publisher in excitement. His answer was disheartening.

"You can't base a book on orbs," he said, sending me to a ghost-hunting book and website that declared orbs to be not floating spirit energy, but dust and pollen particles, water spots and light reflections.

Since I had never found orbs in my photographs before, I went back through my old pictures of Fairhaven for a look.

I've been taking pictures of Fairhaven since about 1985, strictly digital since about 1999. Since my writing and client work requires a lot of photography, I have literally thousands of photographs on my computer of Fairhaven buildings, both inside and out, at all times of the day. One rainy Saturday, I looked through all of them to see if orbs showed up in my old pictures.

There were virtually none. Well, one was very suspicious. The picture I took in 1999 when Finnegan's Atrium had just been built over a vacant lot beside the original Chuckanut Motors building not only featured several orbs, but a large white object by the atrium balcony. I had overlooked it at the time, thinking it was a flash problem. Now that I've had experience with orbs appearing often when psychics are calling them out, I'm not so sure what it is.

While writing this book, I frequently took pictures of the same space many times, only to have just one photo turn up with orbs. Sometimes the orbs were moving, creating a streak. Or they would be in one spot in one picture and another spot the next. They were different sizes and sometimes had color. Some were oblong, but most were round. They could not be seen with the naked eye, but appeared often vividly in photographs.

I looked carefully to make sure that if it were a dust or light reflection, I would cull it from the group. Every picture in this book was taken with a digital camera except for the Wardner's Castle mural.

Though Bellingham Observers of the Odd and Obscure does not consider orbs to be final evidence, they still often coincide with a psychic and measureable investigation including EVPs and EMFs.

The fact that they most often appeared when the Electromagnetic Field (EMF) meters were registering something, says that perhaps they contain energy. The current theory among believers is that digital cameras with a flash seem to be able to capture these anomalies more easily than film did.

After a visit to the Fairhaven Library, where orbs in all sizes appeared by the dozens and seemed to follow us around like puppies, I searched bookstores until I found a book called *Orbs—Their Mission and Message of Hope* by physicist, Klaus Heinemann, Ph.D. and Gundi Heinemann. They explained orbs as "likely not Spirit Beings in and by themselves, but rather emanations from Spirit Beings."

The book also said, "Orbs respond to requests to appear in photographs and will generally not bother showing up in photos when they anticipate their presence will not be noticed".

That made perfect sense to me. My photographers and I had reached a point in our research where all we had to do was ask them to come out and they did! I found I had a knack for knowing where they were even though they could not be seen by the naked eye. We ended up with hundreds of pictures of orbs in Fairhaven buildings, far too many to put in this book and far too many to simply call dust. I've posted many of them on my website, www.hauntedfairhaven.com.

They are small and large, transparent and not, round or oblong. Some contain colors. Some are moving. Psychic, Joanna Schmidt, who attends an annual conference on spirits and orbs, says orbs sometimes contain geometric prints and others appear to show faces.

No photograph in this book has been retouched or Photoshop edited. Some contrasting was done going from color to black and white. Many of these orbs originally contained other colors besides white. Cropping was the other extent of our editing. Because the buildings were dark during the investigations, many of the pictures came out too dark to be printed in the book, even with a flash. Again, find some of them on the website.

If you wish to experiment on your own, visit a place with reported activity, take a few pictures, and then gently ask the spirit occupants to come out. Then shoot again and see what you get. More books on the topic are listed in Resources at the back of this book.

Finnegan's Alley basement, psychic Brian Lee and floating orb.
Photograph by Sherry Mulholland.

An enormous, transparent orb with smaller orbs upstairs in the
Schering Building. Photo by Leslie Smith.

"Haunted Laundromat" Courtesy George Jartos.

6

Literary Spirits

Village Books/Paper Dreams
1200 – 1206 11th Street

Several ghosts appear to inhabit the Village Books/Paper Dreams buildings, especially the downstairs area where visiting authors talk about their books. But they seem to be active in the entire building, even upstairs in the luxurious view condo occupied by store owners Chuck and Dee Robinson. Our investigation discovered shadow figures, orbs and spirits at home in the popular bookstore.

The newer Village Books building on the corner of 11th Street and Mill Avenue was built in 2004, sitting as a vacant lot for many years before that. The former building had been home to a drug store, the Eastern Bakery, Palace Bakery and a Millinery shop over the years. A district historical marker placed there names it as the location of a counterfeiter's hideout in the 1890s.

The Paper Dreams Building, built of sturdy Chuckanut sandstone and brick, was built in 1904 as a grocery store, first the Fairhaven Cash Grocery, and then purchased by Brown and Cole stores in 1923. The Robinsons created the popular card and gift shop, Paper Dreams in the early 1980s.

An upper level above 11th Street was added in the 1970s by then owner, Ken Imus, and now serves as office space for Village Books, with Paper Dreams at the street level and the basement housing part of the bookstore and the space with book readings and near nightly author appearances. This basement over the years was home to Fairhaven Printing and Brentley Softpacks factory and store.

Village Books employees, including Scott Hinkel the night janitor, have reported strange sounds and sights. One night while dust mopping the 2nd floor Scott was startled by "a huge crash" seeming to come from the other side of the bookshelf.

"It wasn't like a 'did I hear something' type noise. It was loud and definite," he said.

Annoyed that he knew he would be cleaning up what sounded like the huge mess of a collapsed bookshelf, he walked around the back to see. While looking at that side the same huge crash came from the side he had just came from.

"And of course," said Scott, "There was nothing there."

He went on.

"Just before this happened, I had noticed a supply closet door wide open. I keep it closed always. And I would have seen it open because it is right next to the elevator that I have to go up with the janitor cart. Also, just then, I found two of the large posters on the floor. They can tip and catch an air pocket and scoot a little ways, but these two had both turned a corner and were a full 15 feet from where they should be."

A few months later while dusting and straightening the pictures on the first floor to second floor staircase, he had another experience with an unseen entity.

"The way I dust them," he said, "is do one side, then straighten them. And I take great care to get them exactly straight. I'm kind of particular about it. Then I do the other side."

After finishing one side, he looked back and half the pictures he had just done were crooked again. "They were obviously crooked, and impossible for me to have missed."

These experiences along with a persistent feeling he's being watched by a man in a dark suit, don't faze him too much.

"I'm very open-minded through meditation and age, and I guess I no longer have a fear about this kind of thing. I just accept it."

With these stories in mind, we went in to have a look.

The Investigation, April, 2012

After a tour of Village Books and the basement book reading area, the psychics in our group began to explore. Sherry Mulholland stayed in the basement, as she said her "spirit guides asked her to sit and meditate".

"I immediately felt the presence of a man," said Mulholland. "I sat in the rocker near the back of the book reading area. Pam (Castanera) and I were trying to capture EVPs (electronic voice phenomenon) when she reported she saw someone in the hallway coming from the staff break room area. Once we realized Linda (the photographer) was upstairs and we were alone, we moved closer to the hallway and tried to communicate there."

Pam Castanera described him as a large shadow passing through the light in the hallway that came from the back room.

"Sherry and I moved over to the hallway area, and continued to ask questions. I then felt a male presence and I was shown a very tall, slight-of-build man probably in his late 30s with short dark blonde hair parted on the side," said Castanera. "He didn't look as though he was from the 1800s though. Sherry said he was more like from the 1930s or '40s. In thinking about him further, I felt as though this man was a very gentle soul and somewhat shy but curious as to whom we were. I felt he was in the corner listening to us talk. Sherry motioned to me that she had seen a man in the shadows by the wall adjacent to us, but he was gone in a flash."

"Looking past Pam I saw him. Front on," said Mulholland. No denying what he was, a shadow person. He darted away as fast as I saw him, heading to the back of the room by the cash register. They (shadow figures) are so fast that to get an opportunity to see one while stopped is a blessing indeed. We worked some more before I asked Pam to join the rest of the team upstairs. I wanted some personal time to connect with the man.

While there I tried my best to get him to communicate with me when I was around the velveteen rocker. No such luck.

Again, nothing was felt, so I moved back out to the rocker in the book reading area and waited for the team. I tried channeling but the men didn't trust the process. I sensed the younger man was a mild mannered, perhaps gay gentleman, who loved the bookstore and how the management supplied the shelves," said Mulholland.

"Neither of these gentlemen died there, but are attracted to the building because of similar interests or perhaps they worked there in the past. There was an older gentleman who wanted me to know that he was a Man, and wanted more machinery downstairs. The younger gentleman likes the cleanliness and orderly displays of the bookstore.

While the older man did not want to be associated with the younger gent, I'm not sure the younger man is aware of the older one, but for sure the elder gentleman is aware of the younger male. They were quite the pair indeed. I believe the older gentleman was connected to the printing business."

Castanera continued.

"The second part of the investigation was upstairs in the Paper Dreams store, with very low lighting. Chuck Crooks (psychic) and I made our way to the back of the store. I wasn't feeling anything at first. There was a lot of shelving and we stopped in an area of books and paper. I immediately felt a presence and started asking questions.

Chuck walked a little bit away from me. I started to feel 'crowded', as if there were lots of beings around me, in a semi-circle. I asked him to come stand next to me, and I mentioned that I started to get goose bumps on my arms, and he said he just started to feel that too. I felt like I was 'seeing things' like small flashes of light, and we both felt like a lot of people were around us. Chuck then said he felt as if he were having 'hot flashes', which I did not feel. Elena Stecca (psychic) came up about that time, and we all walked back downstairs. I felt as though someone was following me, but that feeling disappeared when we got downstairs.

"I think that both places had a lot going on as far as spirit activity, but I also think that the spirits there may have been overwhelmed with all the attention and questions, and were not really comfortable, but not actually negative, about us all being there. Maybe they were just a little uneasy about us, instead of us being uneasy about them."

Digital EVP recordings captured during the visit by Chuck Crooks contained whispers in the background, including one of a male saying, "close enough".

Photographer Linda Sue Hoofnagle took several orb photographs including one on the main staircase. I also got pictures of a very small, but distinct blue orb floating in front of Sherry and Elena in the author reading room and another of a half dozen orbs between the two women and Chuck Crooks. I've posted some of these on www.hauntedfairhaven.com.

I took a number of photographs of Chuck and Dee Robinson's upstairs condominium, capturing at least one large orb floating above the dining room table. Chuck was skeptical of the photograph, still not convinced about orbs, so we tried an experiment a week later.

Meeting downstairs I gave him my camera and asked him to shoot at least 10 pictures in the residence. I then went upstairs with him and shot 10 of my own. None of his photographs contained orbs. One of mine showed a white, transparent circle on the hallway ceiling. Chuck re-shot that area. Nothing appeared.

It appears Village Books attracts more than "live" readers. Some of the departed seem to like the atmosphere, as well.

1

The Mystery of Shadow Beings

In investigating Haunted Fairhaven, "Shadow Beings" or "Shadow People" have appeared numerous times to both employees of local businesses, and to the psychics that search them out.

In contrast to the more benign floating white "Orbs," people seem to be afraid of something dark that moves so fast it is captured only by the corner of one's eye. For many, shadow people are more felt than actually seen. Skeptics say it's our mind playing tricks on us.

Our ghost hunters have seen or received reports of them at Village Books, Dos Padres Restaurant, Finnegan's Alley, Sycamore Square and other Fairhaven buildings. They appear and disappear so fast it's easy to tell yourself it was nothing. One theory says that they are actually the shadows of people having out-of-body experiences, but whatever you believe, they seem to be common in Fairhaven.

Bellingham psychic, Brian Lee, who often sees the deceased, has had many experiences with shadow people. As a psychic security guard, he has a more challenging position, dealing with two worlds at once.

"Some people think of Shadow People as dark, ominous, menacing, portentous and just generally negative. From what I've seen and heard, I have little reason to believe they're of any danger," said Lee.

He notes that they seem to appear mostly as "Shadow forms standing or flitting by quickly, taking the forms of slim, tallish humanoid figures or even vague animal shapes."

"If anything, they're curious, shy, not confrontational and maybe even mischievous, but not quite the bogeyman people may think of them."

Lee acknowledges that darkness itself "doesn't hold much evil association" for him and that, as a psychic, he concerns himself more with the "figurative metaphorical darkness in the human mind or soul, than I would give any worry over these beings".

He describes Shadow People not as dead or alive, but as an "interdimensional bleed-over."

"Our reality is a thin layer of multitudes of continuity happening within the same relative space and time. I believe every now and then a section of it will overlap like some great tectonic plating in the totality of existence, that folds over and peels back, revealing something we normally don't accept into our consensual paradigm."

In Fairhaven, Lee has both seen and heard stories of the appearance of Shadow People. As a Security Guard of many years, much of it doing nighttime surveillance, he's experienced it first hand.

His first Fairhaven assignment was guarding the new condominium construction area across from Starving Sam's and along Old Fairhaven Parkway, and then was transferred to the Harris Square project on Harris Avenue between 9th and 10th Streets.

"Shadows were reportedly seen in windows," he said. "And noises of footsteps in abandoned upper floors kept me and the overnight cleaning staff plenty mentally occupied," Lee said.

"We were even led on a merry chase to the sounds of two separate loud crashing clattering noises that sounded like the pallets of aluminum extrusions had been kicked over, only to find that both times, in separate buildings, that the pallets and building supplies were still neatly stacked and intact."

On another night, he sighted a green flare-like light that fell at a gliding speed and diagonal trajectory towards the bay from a nearby hill, but says it "could have been someone playing around with a signal device".

After spending some time in other parts of town, he was assigned once again to Fairhaven for a patrol and access control assignment at the shipyard at the foot of Harris Avenue. It was there, he said, that things "got about three times as interesting paranormally."

"Our task, as we sat in the shack and filled out our activity logs, was to assure that all staff signed in and out as needed, to decide if they had any business being there, and to open the gate without delay. Numerous times we heard footsteps or shuffling in the gravel, leapt from our seats to attend to the gate, and annoyingly found no one anywhere nearby.

Out on patrols we sometimes saw tall vertical shapes whiz by in front of us or a small otter/raccoon animal shape skim by on the ground without a sound. One guard in particular, (name omitted to protect the embarrassed), did not like the Shadow Person there and I think it sensed it as well, taking a proportionate and counteracting mischievous liking to being around him.

It even went so far as to "buzz" the shack while he was in it, visibly zipping through it at a high speed, flipping up the papers of the logbook."

This would lend credence to the theory some psychics have about Shadow Beings feeding on fear and repelled by positive thought. The topic is often a hot topic on paranormal radio shows, where shadow people are sometimes described as having "glowing red eyes."

But, Brian Lee isn't afraid of them. He says he's got enough stories to fill up a book, but he's comfortable with them.

"I believe they will always be with me," he stated.

8

Ghostly Parties of Finnegan's Alley

The Chuckanut Motors Building
1104 – 1106 Harris Avenue

Spirits keep the party going in the basement of Finnegan's Alley, home to many restaurants and nightclubs from the 1970s through 2012. An investigation by psychics in 2012 found plenty of action going on long after dark in a space that was, at that time, vacant and up for rent.

On the corner of Harris Ave and 12th Street, Finnegan's Alley stands out by its odd shape. Not a tall square brick square like the oldest buildings of the district, it has a curved roof, belying its history as a the 1920's Kulshan Motor Company, an automobile dealership and garage. Chuckanut Drive had been recently paved and tourists wound their way along the curvy, narrow cliffside road from the Skagit flats to Fairhaven.

By 1924, the business had been purchased and renamed Chuckanut Motor Company, specializing in car repairs. The lot on which it sat once held five wooden buildings left from the "boom" era of the 1890s, which burned all to the ground in 1908 when Fairhaven Coffee & Tea's roasting machine caught a wall on fire. No deaths were reported in the fire. The land sat empty until the garage was built.

In 1905, at 1006 Harris, now the entrance to Finnegan's Alley, Fairhaven Meat & Produce Co, Inc. hung raw meat outside for passers-by to access.

Fairhaven Meat & Produce Company at 1106 Harris Avenue
with owners Louis & Joseph Ederer, 1905.
Photo courtesy of Whatcom Museum.

Next door on Harris Avenue, Fred Fisk, ran the Star Market, selling groceries and meat. Historian, Gordy Tweit said that one day Fred went home craving something sweet and dropped dead of a heart attack.

The lower basement area of the Chuckanut Motors building, has seen a lot of businesses since serving as a miniature golf place in the 1930s and then a Royal Crown Cola bottling plant. By the time Phyllis McKee purchased it in the 1970s it had been vacant for a while.

McKee rented spaces to Gallery West in 1972 on the corner upper level and small shops in the rest of the spaces, naming the building "Finnegan's Alley," after Fairhaven's famous turn-of-the-century pharmacist. In 1976 The Fairhaven Restaurant opened in the basement floor.

The 1980s were wild in Fairhaven. Though a class clash was building between the blue-collar workers of the boat and fish industries on the waterfront, rednecks, hippies and the graduates of the university, there were bars and taverns to suit everyone. Dos Padres, Venus Pizza, Cal's Tavern, and others catered to the beer drinkers, while The Fairhaven and Le Chat Noir became the places for cocktails and cocaine.

The frenzy of that era culminated in a big cocaine bust that took place in both "yuppie" watering holes, ending a lot of the fun. The blue-collar taverns were mostly closed by 2000, except for the bar at Dos Padres, which remains active today and attracts nearly everybody.

In Finnegan's basement, The Fairhaven Restaurant became the Fairhaven Pub nightclub in the 1990s, featuring bands and disc jockeys and dancing nightly. As the nights became rowdier again, the stories filtered out of ghost activity.

The disc jockey reported seeing a ghost as a blurred reflection in the glass door at closing. The manager received a gentle hug and reported that in September of 2002, as she spoke to a plumber in the bar, the television came on by itself. She mentioned the ghost and it went off. Customers reported hair pulling and the discomfort of being watched in the restrooms, but often people were so inebriated their reports weren't reliable. When the Fairhaven Pub closed in early 2012, we brought in a group of psychics to check it out.

First Investigation

In late March, psychics Pam Castanera and Chuck Crooks, and photographer, Leslie Smith, spent part of a night in the Finnegan's Alley basement with digital recorders, cameras and EMF meters. The open ceiling electrical tended to set the EMF off, so they were careful to take test readings often.

A back storeroom offered up some chilled spots, but no photographs, while the infamous restrooms contained the largest orbs we've seen in pictures. While both restrooms made the EMF meters go crazy, the men's room showed two enormous orbs moving about, generally near each other. They were caught on a digital camera by Leslie Smith. The women's room had one the same size and was likely one that had moved from the room next door.

There was no voice contact that night, but the recordings seemed to register footsteps extremely close by. The team is always careful to wear soft-soled shoes to avoid contaminating the recordings. Although there were parties dining upstairs at the Big Fat Fish Restaurant, these noises were right next to the digital recorders. Something still inhabited the basement of Finnegan's Alley. Plans for a return investigation were noted.

Second Investigation

Feeling like they hadn't spent enough time in Finnegan's Alley, another new group from Bellingham Observers of the Odd and Obscure went in Friday, April 13th, 2012 to find the spirits attached to those orbs. Psychic, Brian Lee, saw a shadow figure very close by him on the stage and captured some B or C class (not very clear) EVP recordings. Noise from the Big Fat Fish restaurant upstairs made it hard to distinguish voices or footsteps.

Lee also felt the presence of a Longshoreman named Harold sitting at the bar in overalls and a knit cap.

Psychic Sherry Mulholland, channeled the spirit of a young woman in a white dress, weeping uncontrollably for her lost child and husband. She said her name was Marilyn.

"Once it came time to channel, my guides instructed me to focus on the hallway leading out the back door, by the gentlemen's bathroom facility. Linda, our photographer also was pulled to this area," said Mulholland. "The presence of a woman named Marilyn came to me. Just as I was attempting to pull her energy closer a gentle hand cupped my ear and fingers lightly touched my hair and head behind my ear in a loving intimate gesture. It felt endearing.

Marilyn's state of mind was of a woman stricken with grief and unable to speak with us. Linda brought up a thought that rang true to me, that perhaps she was attracted to the building due to counselor's offices there and working through her grief. If that is the case, there is a lot more work to be done."

Indeed, there are a number of counselors in the attached new wing of Finnegan's Alley.

Mulholland went on:

"Marilyn was stricken with so much grief over losing her child and the father having left her alone to deal with it all. She was wearing a white dress with A-line contours, lace indicating a mid-length party dress or perhaps a wedding dress."

"I believe there are so many reasons spirits may chose to stay on, this is one of my theories that may explain Marilyn. The dress and her appearance may represent a time that she holds strongly in her thoughts and is still trying to work through. This traumatic time in her life may have caused her to choose to return or stay on and continue grieving. She looks younger. Maybe she chose to be in her wedding or party dress. She may have had some attraction to the building or a past experience there. She might have worked there or had a business in one of the many shops, causing her to return."

Photographer, Linda Sue Hoofnagle, added, "She feels sort of caught in between dimensions—locked in utter despair. Someone might want to go there and tell her it's OK to go to the brightness because she sure needs it!"

In the kitchen Brain and Sherry had asked many open-ended questions in hopes of getting a response on their recorders. Brain captured several EVP recordings, that of a child saying *"Hello,"* and later of a man saying, *"touch him,"* and just after that, *"told ya."*

"Were the spirits wanting to touch us?" Speculated Mulholland. "The pulling of hair might be from the young child that said *"Hello"* to the team."

Mulholland had made contact with a spirit who lovingly caresses people and "Brian's EVP *"told ya"* perhaps was a response to ghosts' inability to make him aware of them? Only the spirits know their intent for sure."

Mulholland took at least two-dozen photos showing orbs, many in multiples, including one with a large blue orb on Lee's chest, which I've posted on www.hauntedfairhaven.com.

They also felt the presence of a man who kept his distance.

Two months later, in June, I was dining with photographer Linda Sue Hoofnagle and a friend on the 12th Street side of Finnegan's Alley in the Big Fat Fish Restaurant. Although the place was packed with customers, I turned on my EMF Ghost Meter for fun. It went immediately to red and began flashing.

I strolled around the bar and it repeatedly showed electromagnetic activity. The ceiling there is open, and thinking the reading might be from the lighting, I placed the EMF on the floor by our table. It got even more intense. I went into the restroom and it stopped, not going on again until I emerged.

Office manager, Anna Williams, who had recently lost her husband, C.B. Williams, joked that maybe he was visiting us. The former war hero and pilot for Air Force One in the 1960s had often come into the restaurant. We all knew him well.

Linda Sue took some photographs. Later that night she emailed them to me. A group of small orbs floated near the ceiling and wall where we were sitting. Someone or something was in the bar, even at that busy hour of the evening.

Finnegan's Alley remains a mystery with visitors who aren't ready to leave, and not just in the basement.

9

The Spirits of Chinatown

At the foot of Harris Avenue

Chinese workers came seasonally to Fairhaven to run the salmon canneries, and though the Chinatown barracks are long gone, locals have
fond memories, empty opium bottles and the visions of the spirits that
still flit along the rooflines of the marine buildings along the waterfront
at night. Walk along Harris Avenue from Marine Park to the Train station on a warm summer night and you might smell incense and opium,
noodles and chicken. You might just see a shadow person or hear the click
of gaming tables.

In the boom days at Pacific American Fisheries, 501 Harris Avenue
was the site of a large bunkhouse behind what is now a sporting goods
shop, housing several hundred Chinese laborers. Two hundred feet further up Harris Ave was Sam Low's opium den, which catered mostly to
Caucasians.

According to articles in the *Fairhaven Times* in 1900, and the *Reveille*
in April of 1902, the Pacific American Fisheries canning factories grew
so quickly that in 1897 sixty Chinese arrived to work in Fairhaven. By
1899, 600 came from Portland, Oregon, to work the fishing season. Two
hotels near the water, former brothels, the Saint Luis Hotel and the Focal
City Hotel, served as their lodgings until the bunkhouse was built. Two

houses next to the Saint Louis Hotel were Japanese bordellos in the early 1900s, near where the ferry dock sits now.

Goon Dip, a popular local man and entrepreneurial type, found his calling organizing and procuring his countrymen from around the northwest to come to Fairhaven and work the seasons. It was a good arrangement for all and he functioned as the PAF canning contractor for over 20 years.

Historian, George Hunsby colorfully described the residences of the new little Chinatown in his book *The Birth, Death and Resurrection of Fairhaven*.

"This arrangement worked quite successfully that first season and the Chinese soon made themselves at home by setting up their gambling games and opium smoking outfits, all of which were moved over to the new building the following season."

"That was the last time the old sporting houses had human inhabitants. From then on that old area of iniquity where men had been known to be robbed, rolled, and even shanghaied, passed into oblivion, and today not even the rotting timbers remain."

Hunsby described the bunkhouse as a three-story building, housing about 500 people, with the "pleasant" smell of opium floating in the hallways. He bought noodles at their main floor restaurant for 10 or 15 cents per bowl and enjoyed the hot tea they served all day for the workmen. The Chinese men wore long hair down the middle of their backs, and loose clothing. Rarely a woman was there, and they usually suffered from the crippling custom of bound feet, created to make their feet tiny and attractive, but in reality, a painful, debilitating deformity.

An *American-Reveille* newspaper article in 1908 graphically described the bunkhouse during the empty off-season months, when the Chinese workers had gone back to their homes in San Francisco, Portland, and Vancouver, B.C. This quote was reprinted in the *Fairhaven Gazette*, published by historians Penny and Ty Tillson in the fall of 1992.

"In the deep of the night, white objects flit to and fro before the empty-looking windows and strange noises are said to have been heard within the building. In its dark narrow halls and passages ghosts hold nightly revelries and during the day seagulls refrain from lighting on the buildings but go flying over and around it screaming as if in terror. At least these are the facts according to seamen who have made this port many times.

"These strange happenings and weird scenes are more frequent since the Chinese have left and have begun to attract the attention of several south Bellingham (Fairhaven) citizens who have happened to be around the cannery at night. When the Chinese were there, the building was always lighted at night. The Orientals were busy in their secluded dens, playing their mysterious games. When the Chinese left, each one left one of his spirits in the bunkhouse to hold his position until he returned in the spring. Many people believe it is these strange myths of the dragon that make the bunkhouse so dreary.

"On the upper floors rodents are said to scamper across the floor and chase others up and down the winding stairs. White mists which credulous persons say float out and in at the windows are the spirits dancing on the roof, keeping time to the mournful beats of the buoy bell which sounds like a knell in the stillness of the night. As soon as the gray streaks of dawn begin to fret the clouds, these phantoms glide with silent steps in long procession over the tops of the canneries and disappear into the gloomy shadows of the silent bunkhouse.

"It is said that a lonely man who lost all his money in the games of the bunkhouse still wanders through halls and dark garrets, killing rodents to support the spark of life until spring when his fellows return. This old Oriental often ventures to the street but never wanders far from the bunkhouse. His condition has worked upon the sympathy of many people in the neighborhood who have given him coins, but he refuses to spend them even in the support of life. Lately this old man has not been seen on the streets and many think he has wandered into the darkest recess of the dreary bunkhouse and died and that the strange phantoms which haunt the buildings are evil spirits who have come to rob Confucius of his soul." *American-Reveille, 1908* (Tweit Collection)

An opium den for whites sat near where the train station is now, and for many years after, scavengers and treasure hunters in the area dug up colorful opium jars. Despite the abandonment of the area by the busy brothels and Chinese, spirits seemed to become active around 9th and 10th streets when new construction began in Fairhaven 100 years later.

Psychic, Brian Lee, who worked as security at night on the Fairhaven waterfront shipyards and during construction of the new condominium buildings up on 10th street, had many strange occurrences.

"Another guard and I were at the foot of Harris Avenue saw a misty white shadow figure, almost like a snow angel, zip across a roof between the ferry terminal and Marine Park. It whipped through the guard shack at the gate, flipping a page of our log," he said.

He describes loud noises during his nightly graveyard shift at the 10th Street construction site, but he and other guards would investigate and nothing would be amiss.

"There was definitely something there," he said.

To experience the goings on of the Chinatown ghosts, wander the area from Padden Creek to the Train Station, Ferry Terminal and down to Marine Park after dark. They may appear flitting along the rooflines and blowing your coat open in their enthusiasm.

10

Deadman's Point

The shoreline strip at the foot of Harris Avenue where Marine Park now sits was originally known as "Deadman's Point" holding special significance to the Fairhaven area as the location of the original cemetery. Once a bluff overlooking the bay, and a good viewing location for incoming ships, it was flattened out for easier commercial access from the water and the graves moved. Unfortunately, the process didn't really take care of the problem of the spirits that remained. A walk along the beach after dark is sure to raise the hair on the back of your neck.

To enhance the problem, the area from the water up to 4th Street was, over the centuries, home to numerous deaths by everything from ancient battles to more modern shootouts, simply multiplying the supernatural activity.

According to historians, Tyrone and Penny Tillson, in their *Fairhaven Gazette* magazine, the modern 4th Street and Harris Avenue parking lot for the Alaska Ferry was once the scene of one of Fairhaven's biggest shoot-outs.

One night in 1902, Bad Bud Cox decided to rob Butch's Saloon and in the gun battle, two men were wounded and one was killed. Bad Bud got 20 years. After his trial he stated, "I'm glad the witnesses are all young so that they will live until I get out of the pen and can kill them."

Next to Butch's Saloon was the Monogram. The saloon's windows were sucked out when 20,000 pounds of dynamite accidentally exploded down near where the Fairhaven water treatment plant now sits. The Junction Bar and Sample Rooms beside The Monogram served up Bellingham Bay Beer for 5 cents and had rooms to let upstairs. It is now the ferry parking lot.

The Junction Bar at 400 Harris Avenue, 1905.
Photo courtesy of Whatcom Museum.

"After WWI a barber set up shop between the sites of the Monogram and Junction Saloons and gained a reputation as the Bedspring Killer. Several years earlier he had tired of his wife and shot her dead as she lay sleeping in their bed. He took a nap and then stuffed her body into a hollow tree stump. Eventually she was found and the barber sent to the state penal colony. At his trial it had been pointed out that when he cleaned up his sleeping quarters he had neglected to wipe down the bedsprings and long ropes of coagulated blood still dangled beneath the bed." (*Fairhaven Gazette*)

Historian, George Hunsby, born in 1898, whose family arrived in Fairhaven in 1910, described the graves at Deadman's Point. "No one was certain if they were graves of whites or natives, but the most prevalent supposition was that it was an old Indian burial ground. Indian lore presented a story of a great battle fought near the mouth of Padden Creek, between the Lummis and Haida raiders from the north, and that tale may have given rise to the belief that Deadman's Point was an Indian burial ground."

WSU Archeologists have dated the Indian encampment in Fairhaven back to 1500 BC, according to Penny Tillson, historian, so the cemetery may indeed have been ancient.

Psychic and researcher, Sherry Mulholland describes the beach area in her website, www.BellinghamBOOO.com, (the Bellingham Observers of the Odd and Obscure).

"Little did I know before recently that a quiet beach park overlooking Bellingham Bay was once a pioneer graveyard. This same beach was also the site of an Indian massacre. Long before records were kept, a graveyard lay alongside the shore off of what we now know as Marine Park.

"From the writings one would have hardly thought that our forefathers gave a second thought to the bones that lay resting there. Their remains were to be moved to newly existing graveyards, but later bones and coffins were popping up as a reminder of development taking priority over spiritual rest."

Here's what two newspaper articles had to report:

"Bodies Found At Deadman's Point," *The Bellingham Herald*, April 14, 1904. "Coffin Uncovered by Men Engaged in Washing Away the Bluff —Many Legends of the Place. More Evidence came to light this morning that the change of name from Dead Man's (sp) Point to Commercial Point marks an actual transformation now taking place at the historic burying ground of Bellingham Bay. With the washing down of one coffin box and the uncovering of another, it was shown that not all the graves were found when, soon after the town of Fairhaven was laid out in 1899 [must mean 1889], the human remains buried there, so far as they could be located were removed to the cemetery."

Unfortunately, the article went on to say that coffins still remained on the site after the move and were washed down into the water with the force of the hydraulic stream.

"Several skulls an parts of human skeletons" were washed out into the bay. The coffins then uncovered were buried some distance back from what was the edge of the old bluff.

"Very little evidence of human remains could be found from the first box that was washed down, this morning, although this was probably due to the general scattering of box and everything else in that vicinity by the force of the hydraulic stream."

In addition to the fact that the bluff was used for a common burying ground in this vicinity during the pioneer days, there are numerous legends in connection with the point. One of these is that a fierce battle once took place there between Indian tribes, and the slaughter that resulted gave origin to the name 'Old Army City.' Another one is that a ship once sailed into the harbor, many years ago, with a terrible contagious disease among its crew, and that those members who escaped being but a few of the number, buried their stricken mates under the sod of the overhanging point.

It is also stated that in the early '50s [1850s], the garrison of United States troops at Fort Bellingham used the place for a burying ground, taking the bodies across the bay in boats.

"After I moved here from out of state I was drawn to the Commercial Point-Marine Park whenever I was grieving and sang my Indian Songs to heal", said Mulholland.

An article published by the *Daily Reveille* on Sunday, July 26, 1903, talks about the massive hydraulic pump operation, with a one line description, "There is a strange spell about this that seems to rivet the beholder to the spot."

A Bellingham ghost hunter, Ryan Galbraith, recorded an EVP at Deadman's Point of a little girl saying "hello," along with another recording of a calm statement in a native language he didn't understand.

A strange energy also pervades the now vacant lot at 9th and Harris Ave, which will some day be another new building. The trails through the woods nearby by Padden Creek leads to the spot near where pioneer Dirty Dan Harris' cabin once stood, and the scene of a massacre of Spanish soldiers in the 1600s by local natives along the creek. Local legend has it that a Spanish silver or pewter chalice dated 1630 was found by a Mr. Leigh L. Rose, at a depth of about three feet down near 11th Street & Larrabee Avenue.

In the 1930s, there were reports of a suit of Spanish armor complete with a skeleton and knee-high leather boots was found while tearing down Deadman's Point, but if these relics did exist, they have long disappeared (*Fairhaven Gazette*).

The shockingly vivid ghost of a conquistador appeared years ago at the bedside of a family relative sleeping downstairs at the opulent Fairhaven Bed and Breakfast, just beyond the Padden Creek Bridge on 12th Street. Still owned by the Todd family, but no longer open to the public, Kitty Todd related the story. The guest did not know of the ancient massacre in the creek below, but woke to the soldier staring down at her.

Since then there have been many incidents of items being moved about in the mansion, with Kitty placing the blame on the conquistadors who still frequently visit the home.

Bank tellers and bankers at The Nelson Block in 1903.
Courtesy of Whatcom Museum.

ii

The Skeleton Under the Floor

The Nelson Block
1100 Harris Avenue
Foundation built 1891

The Nelson Block, or Bank Building, as it's often called, became famously haunted due primarily to the skeleton rumored to have been found in the basement in the 1970s. Every restaurant tenant for the past 40 years has reported ghost sightings and at one time an actual exorcism was held to try to rid a business of the pesky paranormal activity. The basement has been unoccupied now for many years.

Before completion of this sturdy Chuckanut sandstone edifice on the corner of Harris Ave and 11th Street in 1900, local Indians performed war dances in the open basement space, charging 5 cents apiece, (*Fairhaven Gazette*, summer, 1988). A fence was installed so potential audiences had to pay up.

Owner, Malcolm McKechnie didn't immediately finish the building. Shortly after the foundation laying and Indian dances, Fairhaven's economic boom busted and construction stopped. The foundation was boarded over for ten years. James Purdy Nelson then purchased the corner from his fish trap sale for $9,000, and architect William Cox designed the ornate two-story structure.

Citizen's National Bank became the first tenant, originally known as Henry, Andrews & Co., along with The General Saloon on 11th Street and Ira Shey's Clothing Store at 1102 Harris Avenue. The safe remains in the bank space, which has had many tenants including Video Depot. It is currently an upscale clothing boutique.

The upper floor was a residential hotel with the front corner window and rooms reserved for Mighty Mike Earl who owned and ran the huge saw and shingle mill. He often sat in the window overlooking the busy intersection of 11th and Harris. Sometimes at night, he can still be seen viewing his domain from beneath the arched sandstone framed window.

The basement then housed the Sharpless Barbershop and Baths and Sharpless & O'Dell Billards Parlor.

"Working men arriving downtown from the forest, railroad or waterfront where in ripe need of hygiene and the barbershop would provide complete transformation with a shave, haircut, bath and heady fragrance."
~ *Jeff Jewell, Whatcom Museum Historian.*

By 1902 there were seven barbershops in Fairhaven, much to the relief of the better-bathed citizenry. A shave ran 15 cents and a haircut, 25 cents.

For a time, the (Fairhaven) *Evening Herald* was printed there and then the post office moved in. Professional offices occupied the second floor, as they do today.

By 1972, the building was derelict, according to sign maker, Bill Lynch, who occupied the retail space on the Harris Avenue side, sharing it with the Sur Lando Taco shop. Before he moved in, the space was used as storage for pinball machines for Hart Novelty.

"There were a lot of people living on and off in the building then," said Lynch, including his business partner, who slept in a loft above the shop. Bank Books occupied the corner space and J.B. owned Toad Hall, a pizza place in the basement. Jerry Burn's print shop was in the 11th street shop.

Lynch's room was in back of his shop and he reported hearing steps at night, "crashing, thumping and stomping". But then, he notes that it may have been the wino named Whitey that lived upstairs at the time, but Whitey was missing fingers and walked with a cane and didn't stomp. Earl lived upstairs, too. According to artist, George Jartos, who lived for a while in the basement, Earl and Whitey hated each other and didn't speak.

"There was a large bathroom upstairs with chain pull toilets and funky showers, no tub," said Lynch. The basement was always creepy, dirt floors and sandstone walls. I didn't go down there much."

"A guy named 'Michael the Archangel' lived in a refrigerator box with 10 dogs in the vacant lot next door. He showered in our building, too."

Jartos lived and worked for about 6 months in the basement, which he says was filled with storage. There wasn't any heat so he wasn't charged for electricity and he slept in a little room with a loft bed.

"It was creepy," he said. "The whole place was so old. I heard noises at night but didn't know what they were. There weren't any rats in there."

When preservationist and developer Ken Imus purchased the building in the 1970s to renovate it, the surprised tenants were evicted. The newly remodeled spaces eventually became homes for new restaurants and retail and no one actually lived there anymore.

According to Penny Tillson, publisher and editor of the *Fairhaven Gazette*, the basement once had an exorcism. At the time Speedy O'Tubb's, a busy bar then located in the basement, was having ghost problems.

"For twenty years rumors have floated on the night winds of Fairhaven whispering that the location of the present day Speedy O's is haunted. A female specter could be seen at night as a moving shadow and noises could be heard where none should be.

"These events gave rise to the belief by some that the site was cursed and that any business which opened there was doomed for failure. The employees of Speedy O's, having to work under the aura of this disembodied spirit, decided to consult with an exorcist whom they contacted through the *Psychic Times*.

"Weeks later four women met at Speedy O's to perform an exorcism. The exorcism was completed by the bewitching hour of midnight and an appeasement was buried in the wall near where the human bones were discovered. The ghost now rests soundly in the arms of Mr Death. So Far."

Before Speedy O'Tubb's Rhythmic Underground was vibrating the walls in the basement of the Nelson Block, a generation of restaurants rotated through the space. They included Spats, Digs Inn, The Hunt and the Nickel Bank. Something all these eateries had in common, besides closing down, were reports by employees of an eeriness (or more) in the same general area. It seems the elegant structure built in 1900 had the embarrassment of a ghost in the basement.

The answer to this mystery might be buried in the happenings of nine-ty-two years ago, but the legend has been growing for only the last twenty years since something was unearthed in the first restaurant on the site in modern times, Toad Hall.

"A drain problem was bugging Toad Hall owner J. B. in about 1970 and he decided to tackle the floor with its varying thicknesses of concrete to dig up the buried drain and clean it out. He started shoveling and ran into some 'really rich hummus' under the floor. J.B. is a gardener, the founder of the Fairhaven Garden Club, in fact—and he knows hummus isn't likely this far below the topsoil line."

"It was like garden-quality soil," he says.

"Then he unearthed some tiny bones—'digit-sized bones.' He sud-denly felt that he should stop before looking any farther, so he replaced the bones and closed up the hole."

Were they human fingers? Animal bones? No one knows, but varia-tions of his discovery story multiplied through the years. J.B. says he's not superstitious and the rational part of him still doesn't want to enter-tain the notion of a haunting, but another part of him felt the uneasiness of things moving around. He no longer will talk about it. It has never been dug up.

"The location of his find is toward the south wall, about the middle or maybe a little west of middle, of the antique bar, and approximately fif-teen feet out from the wall," according to the *Fairhaven Gazette*.

"Over the years several people who have worked late in the vari-ous basement restaurants have told the *Gazette* about their encounters. The spirit seems to be (to have been, if the exorcism took), a woman, not threatening as much as unnerving. One man, painting until the wee hours, felt a caring but firm female presence 'telling' him to go home now he'd worked long enough. He said he didn't see anything, wasn't sure he believed, but he 'made like Jackie Gleason, and Awa-a-ay we go'!"

When the "Tap Room" inhabited the basement, there were tales of the ghost of a woman that appeared around 3 or 4 a.m. outside the restroom doors in the foyer.

The Autumn, 1986 *Fairhaven Gazette* reported a new restaurant, "Digs Inn" going into the space. They were also dealing with the ghost of a woman in the foyer.

Fast shooting orb in the basement of the Nelson Block Bank
Building. Photo by Linda Sue Hoofnagle.

The Investigation

These stories in mind, a group of psychics lead by Sherry Mulholland,
from the Bellingham Observers of the Odd and Obscure (BOOO) visited the basement in March, of 2012 with cameras, electromagnetic field
detectors and digital recorders for a two-hour stint after dark.

It was a quiet, cold evening in Fairhaven when we locked the group
downstairs and my husband and I took building owners, Brad Imus
and his wife Jean, to dinner across the street at Skylark's Hidden Cafe.
Frankly, I was too scared to go into the basement. I had been there before
and the heavy, dark energy frightened me.

Since I opened The Colophon Café in 1985, I'd heard rumors about the
bank building. Jacquie, who started the red bus fish and chips restaurant
on the corner, told tales of seeing figures in the hallway by the front door
when she entered the building to use the restrooms.

Brad is as skeptical as his father Ken has always been about ghosts in their buildings. He's never encountered one, and would probably prefer that other people didn't spread rumors, but he is good humored about letting people have a look.

After a couple of hours, our dinner party went to retrieve the psychics from the unheated concrete basement and see what they found.

Pam Castanara and Sherry Mulholland related a conversation with a child who made the electromagnetic field (EMF) meter jump with energy. He seemed to be about 10-years old. When asked by psychic Brian Lee if he knew he was dead, another spirit energy, soothing and adult, seemed to gently remove the child and no more EMF readings were had.

A photograph by Linda Sue Hoofnagle, taken in complete darkness, seemed to show a fuzzy image of a curious child peering around the corner of a post. Since it wasn't clear, we kept it aside, but you can find it on www.hauntedfairhaven.com. There were also several shots of floating orbs. No sign of the entity that frightened so many restaurant employees or the owner of the buried skeleton.

The most dynamic thing that came from the camera was a picture of a fast shooting orb. All agreed it was a good night for a ghost hunt.

12

Going Postal

1400 12th Street

It was apparent Fairhaven's town fathers didn't consider mail delivery volume to be a potential problem when they were building their boomtown. The first post office opened on July 15th, 1889, with Postmaster, S.H. Keeler at the helm.

The original Fairhaven post office was located on the main floor of the Imperial City House. Photo courtesy of Whatcom Museum.

According to the Tillson's *Fairhaven Gazette*—

"Mr. Keeler originally planned on having the post office facilities in the rear of his shoe store, but within a few months the entire building had been taken over by the post office and he was forced to add an addition onto his building to allow space for his shoe business."

"The growth of Fairhaven's mail grew so rapidly that it was announced in San Francisco that Fairhaven set a record as being the fastest-growing post office in the history of the U.S. Postal Service."

"Assistant Postmaster General Clarkson visited Fairhaven to investigate matters, and upon observing the nightly block-long lineup of men waiting for their mail, he immediately began the paperwork which would authorize the hiring of extra staff."

"Apparently the Postmaster General didn't move fast enough and pressures of the sorting room drove Mr. Keeler to distraction and he was adjudged insane by a court of law after his term as Fairhaven's first postmaster."

Ninety years later, in 1978, postman Eddie Miller began delivering the mail in Fairhaven. He was a beloved fixture in the district until he retired in 2009 at a big party held in his honor at Finnegan's Alley. His friendly demeanor and willingness to do extra things for his customers made him popular and much missed when he left.

Postman Eddie Miller on his last day of deliveries in Fairhaven.

When asked about the ghosts of Fairhaven, he had only one story to tell of his 30 years of work. Eddie is not a big believer in the paranormal, although he says he came very close to death during an accident on a nuclear submarine at the age of 19, he didn't believe it then and he doesn't now. His parents were "God-fearing holy-roller Baptists", but "I came out an atheist for sure." This makes his story all the more frightening.

In 1993 Eddie used to take the mail to Speedy O'Tubb's bar in the infamously haunted basement of the Nelson Block (Bank) building. He could have left it with the other mail at the boxes at the top of the stairs in the vestibule, but he was the kind of guy who liked to do a little more for people and he would walk down the stairs and put the mail on the bar.

"Mail's here!" he would yell to the cook above the din of pots pans and kitchen fans.

Cook would respond, "Thanks!"

One day as usual, he went down the stairs, slapped the mail on the bar and called out. There was no answer above the usual kitchen prep noises. He called out again. There was still no answer, but plenty of noise coming from the kitchen.

He left the mail and ran into the cook halfway up the stairs as he was coming down.

"No one answered in the kitchen," said Eddie.

"No one is down there," replied the cook.

"I think I'll leave the mail upstairs from now on," replied Eddie, and he never set foot in the basement again.

Of all the haunted Fairhaven buildings he entered five times a week for 30 years, including the more famously haunted Sycamore Square, he never had another experience like that, but to this day he has not forgotten the Nelson Block basement.

1890. Casino Theater (left), Tontine Saloon (right). Now the location of Skylarks Café and Arabella Clothing. The Vineyard Saloon was built to the left at 1312 11th Street. The Tontine had "furnished rooms" on the second floor. To the far left out of the picture, sat the Spokane Theater. Photo from Galen Biery Collection, courtesy of Whatcom Museum.

13

The Curse of Devil's Row
Sin, Saloons and Murder on 11th Street

One of the most infamously haunted blocks of Fairhaven has to be the west side of 11th Street between Harris Avenue and McKenzie Avenue where the most notorious saloons raked in the cash in the 1890's, developed a reputation for violence and sin, and were just as quickly gone by 1904. According to current workers and a group of psychics, there is still a lot of spiritual activity going on at "Devil's Row".

The wealthy businessmen who built the town of Fairhaven into a city after founder Dirty Dan had left, seemed to be unprepared for the human toll of such rapid, unregulated growth. Despite the gentlemen's clothing and sophistication in the photograph, these well-dressed men were the exception. With thousands of men arriving monthly, limited lodging, lots of work and money flowing freely, what resulted was an almost completely uncontrolled frontier lawlessness.

According to historian Tyrone Tillson, the sixth man from the left in the picture appears to be Fairhaven's thieving town marshal and tax collector, W.S. Parker, who fled to Buenos Aires one night with $12,000 of Fairhaven's tax cash after telling his wife he'd be back after a short trip to Seattle. There he opened a saloon and between that, and joining the Yukon Gold Rush, made enough fortune to pay the money back, upon being pressed by the Pinkerton Detective Agency.

Though the city fathers, especially Nelson Bennett, had dictated that sin would not be a Fairhaven commodity, the sight of workers spending their hard-earned cash in the nearby town of Whatcom was too much to bear, and the saloons went up anyway.

The workers then spent their money locally on women and booze, while getting into fights and killing each other. The businesses spawned to capture this new money became sleazier as time went on, until the point came that the primitive law enforcement of jail, chain gangs and stocks no longer could contain the chaos. By now there was one saloon for every two hundred Fairhaven residents. The results were predictable.

The *Fairhaven Herald* reported in April of 1890, that Constable John DeFries approached James Douglas of Ireland, leaning against the street railing of Harris Avenue in a drunken stupor. He asked him to move on, and without response, decided to help the gentleman when he collapsed dead to the ground from "chronic alcoholism". Nothing was known about him except his name. He was buried without fanfare.

In November, *The Weekly World* noted, "A gambler named Wood went gunning for a man named Marshall along Devil's Row on Eleventh Street last night, but the fog was so thick that the bullets were wasted. Both men were arrested and Wood furnished bail, while Marshall spent the night in the cooler."

The Casino Theater on 11th Street, where Skylarks Café sits now, opened grandly with the Heavy Weight Boxing Champion of the World, Jack Dempsey, (there was later another Jack Dempsey) in a boxing exhibition against the Middle Weight Champion of Australia, Paddy Gorman. The Casino was packed from balcony to back door exit with paying customers and both the crowd and the boxers enjoyed themselves so much, that the two stayed over a few more days and put on another match at the Spokane Theater, a grand place featuring walls lined with classic paintings and fine glassware. Dempsey and Gorman hit it off and spent their idle hours touring Fairhaven, fishing in nearby Lake Padden, and meeting society.

Across the street from Devil's row, sat the Elsemere Hotel (now the Young building), where John Roscoe, owner of the infamous Trocadero at 706 Harris Avenue decided his "girls' should reside. In exchange for their rooms, all they had to do was "work" a man for $5 each night for the house and they'd get 20% of their take, $2 off the week's rent and the choice of taking to the Elsmere the man of their choosing.

The city fathers looked the other way at Devil's Row activities for a long time, until the scandal regarding ballot stuffing at the Spokane during the December, 1890 elections for Mayor and seats on the city council. The saloons didn't win the seats however, and the Treasurer of the conservative Fairhaven Land Company, E.M. Wilson was elected mayor.

Wilson immediately appointed another Land Company man, and prohibitionist, J.J. Donovan as councilman-at-large. Thereafter, the saloon/ theaters days were numbered, as the media (The Fairhaven Herald and the Weekly World were owned by the Fairhaven Land Company), played up the boxing matches as "brutal fights", and regularly reported on the shootings, pistol whippings, and stabbings in the area.

By Christmas, of 1890, even the *Reveille* newspaper suggested it was time for Fairhaven to "Take Measures."

"The past week has been one of almost continual terror to the citizens of Fairhaven. Almost at the beginning a man was shot down in cold blood, without cause or provocation, in a saloon on the principal street of the city, and this was followed on the following morning by an attempt to kill another man, but the attempt fortunately failed in execution. Night after night the citizens have been held up by highwaymen, and robbed of whatever they had in the way of money or other things of value."

"Yesterday morning at about 1 o'clock, two hobos, who have infected the place, held up a man on Harris Street, but obtained nothing from him. He immediately gave alarm and pursuit was made and the two captured, and they are now in the cooler in Fairhaven."

The Mysterious Unsolved Death of Andrew Tweit

In 2012, Gordy Tweit, the 80-year-old retired pharmacist and former owner of the Fairhaven Pharmacy was working in his archives when he relayed a mysterious story of murder in 1891. As we looked through piles of black and white photographs and talked about some of the stranger incidents in pioneer Fairhaven, he suddenly told a story that was new to me, even after 30 years of district research.

"My great uncle was murdered on 11th Street," he said. "He and his brother had the Vineyard Saloon and in 1891 he was murdered for his pocket watch and a few bucks and then they threw him in the bay."

"The policeman then didn't even have uniforms," said Gordy accusingly. "They said he drowned and never followed up."

"His name was Andrew Tweit. Grandma never talked about him. She just told me I should never go into taverns. Many years later someone gave me a picture of all these Norwegians and told me the story. I have a picture of him in a coffin. He was a good-looking guy."

Gordy is one of the steadiest people Fairhaven ever produced. Born and raised in the nearby Happy Valley neighborhood, he's a teetotaler, famous for his no nonsense pharmaceutical advice, and his gift of taking Halloween photographs of local children and giving them the pictures for free. He's often seen sweeping the sidewalk, or visiting with customers, as his former employee, now pharmacy owner, Robin Johansen, fills orders. Gordy won't even collect the old opium bottles, sometimes found near the Ferry Terminal because "he's not interested in that kind of stuff."

Retired Pharmacist, Gordy Tweit, sweeping out the basement
stairwell at the Fairhaven Pharmacy.
Photo by Taimi Dunn Gorman.

Newspapers in the State Archives, told the story of the 26-year-old's demise.

March 24th, 1891, *Fairhaven Herald*—Andrew J Tweit walks off the Railroad Trestle and Is Drowned

"Between 4 and 5 o'clock yesterday morning a loud scream was heard emanating from the neighborhood of the Heacock Mill. The night watchman at the mill and Officer Teeters both heard the scream and at once started for the place from whence it came. When they arrived at the scene all that could be discerned was a hat floating on the water. The scream and hat gave unmistakable evidence that someone had fallen overboard, and as soon as possible, Marshal Parker procured a boat and grappling irons, and after about five hours of dragging the bay a man's body was brought to the surface.

"The body was brought to J.M. Warriner's undertaking establishment, where it was identified as that of Andrew J Tweit, a laborer and brother to Oscar Tweit, proprietor of the Vineyard Saloon. There are several conflicting theories for the drowning, but the facts seem to justify the theory that it was an accident. Tweit appears to have been walking along the trestle on the footboards and as it was rather dark he failed to notice that one of the boards was missing and it is supposed he naturally walked off into the bay and as he fell he uttered a scream.

"Oscar Tweit, the dead man's brother, believes that he was foully dealt with as when the body was recovered his watch was missing. The police place no faith in the theory of murder, as either officer Teeters or the watchman at the mill would have seen any one who was near.

"Judge Curry summoned a jury last evening and held an inquest but all evidence was not in at the late hour and the jury agreed to reserve its verdict until late this morning."

March 25th, *Fairhaven Herald*—"The verdict of the Coroner's jury stated that the cause of death was accidental drowning. The funeral of the unfortunate man will take place this afternoon at 2 p.m. from J.M. Warriner's undertaking parlors, corner of Mill and 14th."

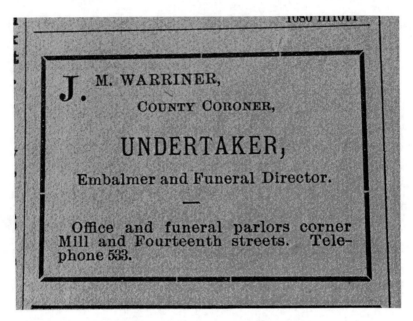

Advertisement in the *Fairhaven Herald*
for the undertaker at 905 14th Street.

The circumstances of his death are suspicious. First, the missing watch reported by his family. Secondly, if someone falls, they usually don't have time for a "loud scream", but rather, a grunt of surprise. At 4 o'clock in the morning in March, it would have been very dark, and the witness hearing the scream may not have been able to see anyone running away.

It is also unlikely any sort of autopsy was done, which might have shown if he had been attacked or struck before he drowned. The underlying assumption seemed to be that he was likely drunk and just fell in, a conclusion that might have prevented further investigation into the death. After all, men were dying daily in Fairhaven of all sorts of things, and probably the town's one undertaker, coroner, funeral director and embalmer was already pretty busy.

Sadly, the Tweits suffered more misfortune, as Oscar's business partner, Chris Christianson died suddenly, followed by Oscar's four-year-old nephew who drowned in a shallow spring well at 1505 Harris Avenue, where the Palace Restaurant sat. Sorrowfully, Oscar went on a drinking spree in his own saloon, causing enough damage that he was pulled into Judge Curry's court and fined.

Fairhaven tragedies continued. Early in 1902, three men were gunned down in a shootout in one of the Harris Ave saloons. Weary of the problems on Devil's Row by July 1903, a "citizens committee" was appointed, and its dour-faced, bigoted Secretary, F.D. Yale, reported upon visiting the Casino that:

"...the purquette was filled with about two hundred Dagoes, Chinese, Japanese, negroes and a few Americans, some of whom might pass for respectable people if they could only get the hard lines painted by long suffering conscience, out of their faces.

"A dozen curtained boxes around the balcony contained partly concealed men, women, beer bottles, glasses and cigarettes in great profession and confusion."

He went on to say "...an insult to the Irish race came out in a corset and proved the strength of his mind by breaking a chain of sausage, and received the well merited jeers of the hoodlums. A man played 'Mocking Bird' on a violin in a manner that was worthy of a better place and cause. Several girls of tender years danced a clog in a cloud of smoke and the fume of beer. Two of these girls were about 7 and 10 years respectively. As we looked upon their sweet innocent, childish faces, and then glanced at the brazen, soulless forms of female depravity whose sin scarred faces had sought refuge behind masks of paint, we shuddered as we thought 'here is the beginning and there is the end of life for those little girls.' My God!"

The conservative *Fairhaven Herald* reported, "The Spokane housed the crap pitcher, the tin-horn gambler, the brazen woman of the town out for a jamboree, the hobo and the loafer with a sprinkling of a class that was only bad because of the depth to which whiskey and morphine had flung them."

When Devil's Row finally burned, the fire department declined to risk trying to save it because there was "too much ammunition in the buildings". By 1904, all the saloon and theater buildings had been torn down. The Tontine had been replaced by the brick building now housing Skylark's Café and Arabella's clothing shop.

Psychic Investigation, April 2012

It was dark and raining hard (why is it always a dark and stormy night when we investigate?) when the group of psychic investigators and I paid a visit to Skylark's Hidden Café and Bar at 1308 11th Street, former site of the infamous Casino Theater.

Daniel, the night bartender was finishing his shift. He told us stories of things that move out of the corner of your eye and "banging" dish noises coming from the kitchen area when no one is there. He also reported that many customers and the staff say that the people in the antique photographs in the lower café seem to be "staring at you, following you with their eyes," and that they are always going crooked, even right after being straightened.

As the bartender cleaned up, psychic Sherry Mulholland was drawn to the quiet, empty lower café.

"I moved a chair in the kitchen and spent some time. I was picking up on what I believe was residual energy of excitement of women reading for a play. Perhaps there were rehearsals for the stage. There was lots of emotion indeed. With my psychic ears I could hear women's voices, but my recorder did not pick them up."

Pam Castanera felt the presence of an elderly woman in a downstairs booth, and a strong feeling of "being watched" in the upstairs banquet room above the bar.

Once the café was closed and staff had left, the investigators, including Sherry Mulholland, Pam Castanera, Tracy Schwent, Kandee Young, and photographer, Leslie Smith, settled into a circle by the fireplace to meditate.

Mullholland went on.

"Once I returned to the upper restaurant I asked for the brothers Oscar and Andrew. I asked about Andrew's watch. What I got were their thoughts. Andrew doesn't know what happened on the night of his death. Oscar is very angry believing that Andrew was murdered. He thinks it was on purpose, and that the culprits wanted it to look like he'd been rolled.

Once we all gathered back to the setting area in the wingback chairs by the fireplace we grounded and focused to allow the spirits to come closer for us to work with them. At the end of the grounding I asked them to move the mirrors above Kandee's head. We all watched on in excitement of anticipating their move, alas nothing."

Pam Castanera reported the strange events that happened next.

"No one was getting much on the recorders, and the EMFs were very quiet, so we sat in the comfy chairs and I asked Sherry if she could do some kind of a séance. We did a relaxation exercise with her lead, and got very calm, all five of us. Sherry was asking if anyone would like to join us, and a female spirit did."

She goes on to say that suddenly Tracy exclaimed, "Someone is here. The scent is so wonderful, so sweet!"

Although the rest of the group felt her presence, no one else could smell the fragrance. The spirit stayed "a good while, like 10-12 minutes".

When Tracy didn't feel her anymore, she seemed genuinely distressed that she didn't have the sweet scent anymore, so we kind of came out of the relaxation and started talking about it, said Castanera.

Tracy got up and walked around by the bar, to come out of her self-hypnotic state, and suddenly looked up, saying 'You guys! Look at the mirrors!' (which up till now were all straight, and orderly looking). And, when I looked up, for the love of God, they were all askew! I couldn't believe my eyes. Even the ones that were so high up no one could reach them, were all tilted this way and that."

"I guess we were all so relaxed and with eyes closed, trying to connect with any entity we could, that no one heard or felt or saw the mirrors all tilt during that 15-20 minutes. Tracy then straightened out the ones she could reach, but they never seemed like they were originally, very straight and even. It was pretty cool I have to admit," said Castanera.

Because they couldn't turn off the outdoor music speakers, the group didn't get any clear digital recordings, but Leslie Smith took numerous photographs of floating orbs throughout the restaurant and a shot of the mirrors across from the bar, both before and after they moved.

Before I left early for the night, I got a picture of a small orb sitting on the corner just below the fainting couch on the upper level. It appeared to be surveying the restaurant below. I've posted it on www.haunted-fairhaven.com.

Any night, stormy or not, the ghosts of saloon partiers, gunfighters and painted women remain on Devil's Row and inhabit the mirrors and photographs of Skylark's Café.

Dos Padres during remodel and repainting after the extensive bar fire of 2007. The ghost of a Victorian woman, who the staff has named Stella, is often sighted sitting in a chair beside the upstairs neon signs. Photo by Taimi Dunn Gorman.

14

Something Nasty in the Basement

Dos Padres Building
1111 – 1113 Harris Avenue

Joey has been the bartender at Dos Padres for the past 13 years. Dark-haired, personable and fast-working, customers come just to see her and to drink the potent margaritas she mixes while bantering with bar audience. She also has to work with ghosts daily.

I sat at the bar one night, while the rowdy crowd watched basketball on TV. She told me about the ghosts, and that there was a big fire in 2007, so hot it melted the televisions down the wall. It totally destroyed the 100-year-old bar. The firemen had never seen such a hot fire. The cause of the fire was never determined.

"An insurance investigator estimated damage to the restaurant is about $100,000, said Bellingham Fire Department Spokesman Brian Flannelly," in an article in the *Bellingham Herald*. "Whatever started the fire was consumed by it," Flannelly said. "We can tell you where the fire began, but we can only proceed so far with the investigation without the ignition source."

It was actually the second big fire in the same spot. The first had taken out several buildings in the 1920s. The rebuilt building had three levels, the upper, the basement and the lower, each housing different businesses.

Dos Padres had occupied all three since the 1970s.

The latest fire had burned the framed ghost pictures I had hoped to see. Ghost sightings and experiences in the building were so common they actually posted photographs in the bar.

I had asked Gordy, the pharmacist next door, what he remembered about the old businesses. "Had there been any strange deaths there?"

Gordy replied, "When I came to work here, the third section down was a grocery store and a meat market. The lower part of Dos Padres was the meat market. The upper part first in 1929 Mr. Strand had a mercantile store there. It changed time and time again. They went out of business.

"Benedict Marine Supply went in there. They took up the whole building. All of a sudden I remember. Although he had just quit here, this guy had worked in the Benedict Marine Supply and I was a senior in college in 1952. The *Prelude* went out on a sail and it was rough out. There were three families and their kids. The two girls got sick so they left them off at Fisherman's Cove and went back out. The *Prelude* was never found. Four bodies were found and two were not. He had worked there for a short time before this happened."

While I digested this tragic shipwreck story, he went on.

"One guy had a beauty shop in the basement where Dos Padres is. After the Marine Hardware left it had become three spaces. It was a ladies' beauty shop. He had this young boy working for him that was in love with him and the boy committed suicide. He was about 18 years old."

I asked Phyllis McKee, the owner of Finnegan's Alley across the street, if she remembered the hair salon.

"Yes, I had my hair done there once," she said. "The place where the three windows are in the bar now was the door to the downstairs."

I found an article that said there was a shooting in the basement. Did he die there in the salon? I wanted to find out.

Back in Gordy's basement museum a couple of weeks later, I asked him again about the shooting.

"The salon owner's name was Ned Lowry", he said.

"What year did it happen?"

"I don't know."

Gordy pointed me to his extensive collection of City Directories. I knew it had to be late 1960s or early '70s and I started looking. Sure enough, in 1971 under Beauty Salons was Ned's, 1113 Harris Avenue. His listing was gone by the 1978 issue.

Psychic Investigation, April 2012

These stories fresh in my mind, I gathered psychics Sherry Mulholland and Pam Castanara, historian Penny Tillson, and photographer Leslie Smith to the Dos Padres bar late one rainy night (again with the 'dark and stormy') to explore the places in the restaurant with the most activity.

For years the employees had talked about the energy in the restaurant. Joey the bartender and Debbie the waitress said that psychics have often come by and mentioned the ghosts in the building without being told about them.

A women in a lacy Victorian dress seems to be at an eternal party in the dining room, and the staff has left a chair in the balcony to the right of the front door where she is often seen sitting beside the neon signs. The staff calls her Stella.

"Psychics tell us there is a ghost in a party dress having a good time," said Debbie.

"She sits either in that upstairs window or at table nine," said Joey. "There seems to be this gentle female energy upstairs, but a scary male energy downstairs."

Closing waiters finish their work quickly, not wanting to be down there very long. The site of the former hair salon seems to emanate an energy that scares anyone who goes down there.

Long-time waitress, Debbie Hollingsworth, told me that she had turned down the bartending job, refusing to work late and have to go into the basement alone. She had once seen a black apparition by the salad bar in the dining room that scared her thoroughly. The downstairs energy is even worse. She said one of Joey's friends had her hair pulled one night while waiting until closing. That's happened numerous times.

"How about the parties down there?" I asked Joey.

The space is frequently reserved for special occasions and banquets.

"Oh, they're partying and drunk and don't notice it," she replied. "It's later, when we have to clean up…"

The energy in the downstairs space beneath the kitchen where the restrooms are is milder, she said, although a waiter told me he had just recently found the water running in the sink in the women's room again, the stopper in the sink and no one anywhere around. It had flooded many times, he told me. "Something" likes turning on the water.

"The washer also gets turned off mid-cycle all the time," he noted. "I've seen it."

Now I was sitting in the bar, it was 11 p.m. and the action was still going strong, every seat was packed and the noise was loud. Joey brought me another margarita while I waited for the psychics to come back from the basement. I wasn't hopeful of their return anytime soon. I should be in bed, I thought.

I ordered tortilla chips. I was sitting in the corner of the bar that was once the entrance to the basement, talking to something that probably wasn't there, and taking occasional pictures of the wall in search of orbs. Joey said it was becoming the strangest night she'd seen in a long time.

Back in the 1980s, the Old Fairhaven Association held their board meetings in the basement. I was a member then and remembered feeling vaguely uncomfortable down there.

"Downstairs is just plain scary," said Joey, bringing me my second margarita.

"There's an ominous feeling, doors slam. Upstairs it's lighter energy, although sometimes liquor bottles fly right off the shelf onto the floor," she said.

The bar got louder and I began to feel like the living were more annoying than the spirits in the basement. I dripped salsa on my Mac laptop. Tired, I finally gave up and drove home. The psychics were still in the basement.

A couple of days later, their reports came in. Sherry Mulholland reported a strong male presence, but the noise upstairs in the bar prevented any EVP recordings. In the dining room basement, there was a clear sound of someone crying. Leslie didn't get any unusual photographs, but Penny took a photo showing at least three distinct translucent orbs floating up by the blue ceiling in the basement banquet room.

Pam Castanera felt a distinct male energy in that room.

"Much to my surprise I didn't feel negative energy. I did feel a male energy in the banquet room, but there was nothing 'creepy' about him," said Castanera.

"It was difficult to isolate him because of the high EMF of the room due to the generator and wires in the walls. However, the meter spiked to yellow frequently, but not consistently away from the walls.

"I felt him, but not until the last round we made of that room," said Castanera. "It seemed as though he waited until we were about ready to leave when he finally came through for me. I then did have consistent readings of energy in places that I did not on the first two visits I made to the banquet room. In fact the whole room was energized at that point, which was almost at the end of the investigation, approximately 1:15 a.m."

"At one point I felt he was right in front of me in the center of the room. Maybe he felt safe with us after seeing us down there a couple of times prior to this. I was talking to him, and Leslie the photographer felt him there, too," said Castanera.

"I was asking him the usual questions about his reasons for not moving on, if he had worked there and so on. This went on for at least 15 minutes, but please note that I did not get any EVPs during any time in the investigation. It wasn't until I asked if there was anything we could do for him to help him move on, did he make his quick exit.

"I knew this because as soon as the words about us helping him were out of my mouth, the EMF detector shut down, or went back to no activity immediately, from a solid strong yellow light back down to green with no return to yellow at all. I no longer felt his presence. I interpreted this to mean he didn't want help from us in terms of getting his energy back on his path to the next realm. That was quite clear to me, and also to Leslie who was standing there the whole time. I never did understand who he was or what his prior function there was. He was not a jovial happy energy, but neither was he 'creepy' nor malicious in any way.

"I forgot to mention that when Leslie and I went back down there the last time, I felt a light poke in the center of my back. Leslie was in back of me but not close enough to touch me and she had her hands full of camera equipment," said Castanera.

At the end of the evening, the group sat in the restaurant's front window table trying to make contact with "Stella," with no success. Sherry felt she was nearby and stayed until 2:30 a.m., but Stella didn't make herself known.

About a month after the investigation, I met historian Penny Tillson in the restaurant to talk about the happenings in Dos Padres. We asked the staff about the ghosts, and the waitress mentioned that the music kept turning off by itself.

"Is it Stella?" I asked amused.

The music turned off immediately.

A couple of weeks later I brought psychic, Elena Stecca in for lunch. She sees and communicates with the departed on a regular basis, and I had personally witnessed her doing some amazing work with a suicide ghost haunting an office. She knew things that had been kept very private and channeled his responses to our questions, so I had complete faith in her intuition.

It was the Friday before the busy Ski to Sea festival and Memorial Day weekend of 2012. The staff seemed very stressed. Debbie came by to take our order and told us that things were breaking in the kitchen that were brand new, they'd had problems with the liquor order, the sink downstairs was turning on by itself and scared kids had been running back upstairs not wanting to use the restrooms.

Elena went downstairs to check it out.

"There are two guys down there," she said offhandedly.

We finished lunch and went to the basement with Debbie to confront the ghosts.

While taking pictures looking for orbs, I sternly told them (or the wall) to knock it off for the weekend, and that they were stressing every-one out and they needed to take a break.

"They are giggling," said Elena. "As though they've been called out over it. It's like a joke."

"And you will NOT follow us out of here," I finished, and we stomped up the stairs.

A week later I dropped in to see how it went.

"It got worse," said Debbie. "In fact a couple of days later Joey was tripped while carrying a cash register till down the stairs late after closing and money flew everywhere. She said it felt and looked like a black cat, but there was nothing there."

Spirits still are active in Dos Padres, both upstairs and down. If you're lucky (or not), you may get to meet them.

15

The Castle Ghost

Wardner's Castle
1103 15th Street at Knox Street

This chapter was written by Edward Davidson and Taimi Dunn Gorman.

As with 'Paul Clifford', in Bulwar Lytton's Victorian novel of the same name, 'it was a dark and stormy night' in February of 1999, when antiquarian Edward Davidson arrived in town accompanying an 18-wheeler full of furniture from his three San Francisco shops for his new home on South Hill.

Invited to spend the night at a friend's bed and breakfast, he awakened after a few hours sleep, determined to cross town, flashlight in hand, and find the pile of lumber that was Wardner's Castle. The power was not yet on and the 3-story, 5,000+ square-foot building loomed in the dark, its five-story garret soaring in the mist.

Wardner was said to have garnered $60,000 in fewer than a single handful of weeks in real estate speculation.

"If that's not what thieves do, then my name's not Edward Davidson and I AM Wardner incarnate," Davidson smiles.

"Actually," said Davidson, "Though I didn't want to do it, I knew if I failed to spend the night in his Castle, it would always be his, never mine."

He can't remember now if the sellers in the person of Gloria Harriman, even mentioned "so-called hauntings," as he puts it, but he does remember her saying she sensed Davidson himself was big Jim Wardner reincarnated. She also insisted that the numbers in the sale, factor up to 12, so the final price was $723,000.

"And that was why, when in my San Francisco office, I penned in that number on her penultimate and third counter suggestion of $732,000. I also wrote, 'final bid,' knowing she had no where else to go. She bit," Davidson said. "And the place was mine."

Now deceased realtor and friend, Jim Neal, had tossed him a little real estate booklet from Bellingham, which he caught mid-air on a visit to Fairhaven a few months earlier. It was open to a full-page color aerial photograph of the behemoth. That was the first inclination Davidson had •that he and the house would be intimately involved for a handful or more years. An eccentric idea perhaps, living alone in a 23-room Victorian mansion.

Even so, flashlight in hand, Davidson explored his new abode, knowing instinctively where what antique furniture and which 19th century paintings would go and how each room would be used.

"Rumors of hauntings proliferated, and indeed," Davidson admits, "if any house were haunted, this would be it. Like a good character actor and putting it simply 'it looks' the part." But being a logical man, Edward does not believe in ghosts now, and he didn't then, either. He did have a fright, however.

"The Harriman's had stuffed a life-size portrait of Wardner in a closeted wedge. When I opened the door it tumbled out scaring the hell out of me. I mean it was moving wasn't it?"

Sometime during the night he dozed off on a first floor toilet reading Wardner's own hand-typed autobiography, which the Harriman's had left propped on the dining room mantel. He woke-up missing his glasses. They were on the 3rd floor.

"I'm sure I just dropped them there," he said. "On the other hand," he says reasonably, "there was a difference of two floors between me and m'glasses. I WAS reading and I can't do that without 'em. Well...."

Davidson was certainly not the first eccentric to reside in Wardner's Castle. Wardner himself was extraordinary for his time, an adventurer, entrepreneur, opportunist and storyteller like Davidson himself.

Born in Milwaukee in 1846, young Wardner had all the makings of a businessman early, when at the age of eight he factored the profit in purchasing a pregnant rabbit, breeding, then selling the offspring. This first business was a profit maker, paying for his school books and giving him more spending money than the other boys until the age of 13, when he went to work in a drug store as a clerk and student.

Kids grew up early in those days. His skill as a pharmacist grew quickly and by the age of 17, he was serving as a hospital steward in the Civil War, having gone on the lam due to an accidental overdose of laudanum being administered to a client resulting in death.

"Through no fault of my own," Wardner insisted in his autobiography, stealing a line if nothing else from none other than Julius Caesar, whom after a particular battle in Gaul, reported to the Roman Senate that some legions had been lost.

On the subject of war, Wardner by his own admission was present at the battle of Gettysburg, where another Bellingham denizen had the temerity to make a 'Frontal CHARGE' across the field in an attempt to win the day for the Confederates. Believing the die was cast, for Wardner was nothing if not prophetic, he threw himself face down pretending a fatal position until the tide of confederates had swept over him; and before General George E. Pickett's army was beaten back by the ultimately victorious Union boys, young Jim got up and ran like hell.

Ran, as it were, all the way to what would become Wardner, Idaho, where he came upon a pair of miners who'd struck gold in the hills there. Sharing a bottle of moonshine he happened to be carrying with him, Wardner "drank the pair under the table", as he describes it, and awakened early enough to borrow their hatchet. With it he flagged all the trees in the surrounding area while they slept, and claimed a right to part ownership in their strike. Mining then was not possible without water and Wardner, the fledgling Robber Baron, shrewdly now owned that resource.

The rest of his youth was full of numerous travels, adventures and schemes in frontier towns from Deadwood to Virginia City, which lead to wealth and fame and Fairhaven.

His colorful, unabashed biography is full of exaggerations, but records show he had made and according to him, cheerfully also lost several for-

tunes by the time he came to Fairhaven. A chance meeting on a train with
investor, contractor, and sometime Territorial Governor of what would
eventually become the state of Washington, Nelson Bennett, convinced
him to come to what they together envisioned would become the 'metrop-
olis of Puget Sound' through the peregrinations of the Union & Central
Pacific Railroads. What neither man anticipated however was that Seattle
money would reach the railroad men first.

Characteristically the optimistically inclined Wardner purchased 135
lots in Fairhaven, which were leveraged into business endeavors, found-
ing the Fairhaven National Bank, the Fairhaven Water Works Company,
the Fairhaven Electric Light Company, the Samish Lake Logging and
Milling Company, the Cascade Club, the First National Bank and a coal
mine. In the process he was elected Fairhaven Alderman.

Wardner's ventures proved so successful he reputedly profited $60,000
in fewer than two months. With such profits he built a home; designed by
Kirtland Cutter, and built in 1890.

Wardner's Castle in the mid 1980s. Photo by Taimi Dunn Gorman.

Wardner's Castle as it's now known, is an imposing three-story mansion on South Hill overlooking Fairhaven and the bay. It's comprised of 23 rooms, seven of which are bedrooms, owning seven fireplaces, a sunroom, and from ground level to its top, there's a five-story turret, library and a carriage porch, cum Porte-Cochere. It was the height of luxury and elegance in its day. The view is spectacular.

"Wardner's new residence on Castle Hill is fast assuming vast proportions. It will be the most costly and elegant residence on Bellingham Bay, and one of which the town may justly feel proud. Mr. Wardner is now in the East, where he will purchase the furniture and fittings." from the *Reveille*, 1890.

The *Seattle Post Intelligencer* reported on Wardner in 1899, "...and now he lives in the finest residence in Fairhaven, on a terraced hill, and his house is surrounded by a handsome park, designed by an expert gardener, decked out with rare flowers and herbs. Then he owns the speediest horses in Fairhaven and has a finger in almost every enterprise the town supports."

He noted in his autobiography, "Jim Wardner of Wardner, Idaho," that "modesty never kept me in the background."

"Then," he said, "I started my Cat Ranch."

There is speculation in most quarters that his claim of breeding black cats on nearby Eliza Island for fur was just a hoax, created to placate a desperate young reporter looking for an interesting story, but nonetheless, he wrote a chapter about it in his biography, and cats, especially black ones, populated Fairhaven well into the 1980s. Wardner's unique "Consolidated Black Cat Company" was reported widely at the time in national newspapers.

In 1891, the *San Francisco Examiner* printed an article that began: "A novel company has just been organized on Puget Sound for the propagation of black cats. An island is to be purchased, so that the cats cannot intermix with the blue, gray, white and spotted cats of the surrounding regions, and there the black cat breed is to be perpetuated for all it is worth".

The pelts of these cats, called "hood seals" were reportedly sold to unscrupulous furriers for $2 apiece. However, others believe this was just a story. Upon reading Wardner's biography, castle owner Davidson said,

"He wouldn't have done that. It would have been a public relations night-
mare. You can't tip off your client base to your fraud and get away with it.
And Wardner was no fool. He just took everybody else for one."

A 1951 article in the *Seattle Times* gleefully shared it as the "Weird
Hoax That Stole a Nation's Headlines."

Though it is pretty well known that cats hate to swim, no one has yet
been able to explain the plethora of pure black, and black and white feral
cats that populated Fairhaven years ago, giving rise in the 1980s to The
Fairhaven Kitty Committee. The volunteers cared for the feral strays for
years, providing food, spaying, medicine and adoption, when possible.
They lived throughout the district in "kitty condos" provided by the committee for shelter.

By 1988, it was reported that more than 28 wild cats still lived behind
district restaurants. Most have long since been adopted, but if you look
closely you may yet see a flicker of a fleeing feline off a cobblestone
walkway in Fairhaven.

One of the few reminders of those days is the Black Cat Restaurant in
Sycamore Square, which seems to harbor as many ghosts as the Castle
itself.

Unfortunately, the huge wooden Victorian bungalow was only home
for Wardner and his family for a year. Reverses in business investments
forced the sale of the majority of his Fairhaven property for cash for more
wheeling and dealing; and Wardner traveled the world, but never came
again to Fairhaven.

A photograph taken of Davidson conducting a tour with his favorite
cat 'two-e', who spells his name simply EE, reveals the cat's attention
focused on a wall next to the Mural Bedroom. There's no one there.

"Even so," says Davidson. "And no, I refuse to accept spirits."

A new family purchased Wardner's creation and the legends continued. Owners through the years have reported wandering cat ghosts, warm
spots on the carpet, and the smell of Wardner's pipe tobacco in the halls.
The home has passed through the hands of numerous owners, serving as
a Thursday night Chicken & Dumpling restaurant in the 1940s, student
housing, a bed and breakfast, and a private residence.

So powerful is the legend of ghosts inhabiting the mansion that even
in the 1940s the home was unrentable, until Jim Wynne's father signed on

at a buck fifty a day. Much to the disappointment of the children, nothing happened... at first.

On at least one occasion a visiting relative inquired why the Wynne's didn't leave; then heading for one of the upstairs floors, the family cat stopped unaccountably and with raised hackles paused, frozen before a blank wall, then scrambled insanely between their ankles to escape. The cat screeched, the mother screamed. The children laughed with satisfaction. The mother refused to live there another moment and soon after, the family moved.

After years deteriorating as hippie and student housing, antique dealers Larry and Gloria Harriman purchased the home in 1977 and began a long restoration process that led to it opening as a bed and breakfast.

Taimi Dunn Gorman and her father, James Young, did a photo shoot to accompany her article on the Harriman family and the mansion in the 1980s. Antiques filled every room. Stepping through the door was a trip back in time.

Gloria was a believer in the supernatural and told Davidson stories of cats and pipe smoke, strange footsteps and ghosts. She said that the ceiling in her daughter's room caved in when she stepped out and that the kitchen once caught on fire. Several people, including Taimi's future sister-in-law left the bed and breakfast in the middle of the night from fear of something she couldn't explain.

As to the ceiling of Gloria's Daughter's room collapsing, Davidson says her room was directly below the third-floor bath with 10,000 blue tiles. On one occasion while he was in San Francisco on business, that bath sprang a leak again, leaving six inches of water on the floor of the second story and an inch in the ground floor dining room.

"No disconsolate idle and unemployed ghosts," he said, "just faulty home improvement."

On the third floor the Harriman's commissioned local artist, Laurie Gospodinovich to paint an enormous mural depicting the mansion. The faces of the owner's family and friends, Mr. Wardner and the artist herself, floated in the mist in the foreground. Many viewers found it unsettling.

The mural on the third floor by Laurie Gospodinovich.
Photo by James Alfred Young.

The artist died on August, 22, 1984, at the age of 21 in a motorcycle accident, five years before Davidson purchased the property from the Harrimans. The gifted artist had been set to study in Paris before being struck down by a careless driver at a Bellingham intersection. Few photographs remain of her work.

Undaunted by the mural, Davidson moved in on the Harriman's dust and rumours. Over the years he lived there, visitors reported strange goings on, including Taimi's own family at one of his annual formal New Year's Eve celebrations. Her teenaged stepson vacated the bathroom just off the kitchen, reporting a mist that had entered through one wall and departed through another. A photograph she took of her mother-in-law on a couch in the sunroom shows a mist floating in front of her.

"It was much the same mist," Davidson says, "as the one shrouding the garret that rainy morning in February of 1999."

Davidson was nonplussed.

"When people ask me if it was haunted, I always find out if they believe in ghosts. If the answer is yes, I understand that's because that's what they want to hear about. To this day I still answer the way people want to be answered. It makes life easier when you make your friends happy."

For himself, Davidson advises, "Ghosts and reincarnation are just too good to be true. Delightful dovetailing like the corners of an antique dresser drawer of course, but the idea of life after death is more charming than believable. Unless you're willing to stretch the balloon too thin for it's own good." he said. "And if you do that, the ball of wax so to speak, will always, eventually burst."

For a while Davidson ran the Castle as a bed and breakfast, and says only "four or five people actually left early, before evening, saying they simply couldn't spend the night. The arresting mural probably didn't help." As the walls were crumbling and needed repair, Davidson finally covered them with sheetrock, leaving a cut out so the self-portrait of the artist's face showed through the wall.

That way "someone in the future who may want it uncovered again can open it up as they like."

He did note something he felt strange. The mural on the blue bathroom wall, depicted a young man about 33 years old with a mustache, hanging on to iron railing. "He was a ringer for me," said Davidson. "I don't know who he was. Nor do the Harriman's. Possibly someone Gospodinovitch knew."

He said no furniture moved around by itself.

"Things did get lost, but it was probably just me. Tools vanished like there was no tomorrow, but I always had work going on."

He does admit he did not like going into the basement and would not descend the enormous coal bin stairs after dark.

"There was a part of the basement that had been bricked over and my imagination worked overtime."

He also admits he did smell damp tobacco, which was strange since he has anosmia, an inability to smell. "I identified it because I once smoked a pipe and the musty taste is unmistakable, " but he repeated firmly, "It's not a ghost, even if Jim Wardner did smoke a pipe."

And then there was the night he was awakened from sleep by a loud thumping outside the mural bedroom on the second floor. It sounded like someone rapidly stomping up the stairs. "But," he said, "There were just not enough damned stairs to explain the 45 seconds or so that it went on."

A nervous but driven Davidson opened the door leaving the chain on, to find nothing there. He settled back in, sure that it was just high blood pressure and elevated imaginings.

"I don't believe in ghosts," he repeated.

Eventually, he decided the country was better suited to him, sold the castle for a cool million to a couple with a child, and moved to 10 acres in Everson with a small lake and a maze—where yard statues surround the property like museum pieces cum graveyard manifestations. He still doesn't believe in ghosts.

"Gloria and I are the only two people who've made money on the place," said Davidson. "Even Wardner himself, lost everything trying to keep it; holding on too long. It's almost as if everyone has been waiting for the coming bust, which always comes."

"As they say in the stock market," in which Davidson also has worked, "'Only pigs lose money.' I got out in the nick of time, like those legendary investors who liquidated their positions in 1929 on Thursday the 29th of October, the day before Black Friday. No! I'm no Jim Wardner," he nods in agreement with himself.

The next owner family did extensive renovations, including replacing the old windows. They separated soon though, and the empty mansion lacked a firm hand once again, taking awhile to sell. It is reported that someone acquired it in 2012 for $750,000. It is currently being remodeled. We've heard rumors that the mural has been destroyed, and no one knows what the future will bring to the haunted mansion on Fairhaven's south hill.

"I drove by a few mornings ago," Davidson says, "on my way back from a grocery run. There was a lot of construction in evidence. It was early morning and misty, much like that day in 1999 when I set out on foot with a flashlight, looking for my new house."

16

The Ghost Train

From historians Penny and Ty Tillson

Every December, there are reports of the mournful whistle of the "Fairhaven Ghost Train," rumored to run from Fairhaven through Happy Valley and down to the Skagit Valley. The whistle blows, the wind blasts through, and the roar of the doomed train is heard.

On December 21st, 1892, a freight train left Fairhaven southbound. Earlier, a train of logs had crossed the bridge across the Skagit, and the weight of it had broken the chord above the long wooden span and sprung the bent below. The watchman discovered the break, and a carpenter's gang had been sent up from below Mt. Vernon to make repairs.

The superintendent declared it safe for passage, much to the distress of the foreman. The bridge might be safe in two hours time, but the 'super' insisted the train make the crossing. As it made its way across, the bridge broke and the train tumbled into the river, killing all three men on board.

It is reported by many residents of Happy Valley and Fairhaven that around midnight on the anniversary of the crash, the ghost train runs on a track that hasn't been there for years. It stops at stations that are but a memory, and it clatters on to the Skagit at the wrecked bridge, and the locomotive drops to the bottom of the river… the end of the run.

The Cash Grocery. Photo courtesy of Whatcom Museum.

17

Restless Residents

The Bellingham Bay Hotel
909 – 911 Harris Avenue
Built 1901

Having had a brothel upstairs and a saloon downstairs, the Bellingham Hotel Building has always been a suspected haunt for turn-of-the-century ghosts. When contacted by the owner of the Bay to Baker Trading Company, a travel goods and gift shop at 911 Harris Avenue, my ghost-hunting group was ready to visit.

Owner, Tina Schwindt, noted that the front door had opened by itself on numerous occasions, windy weather or not, and the scent of burning wood in their visitor center wafted through far too often for her taste. Worried about fire, and wondering about the mysterious doorman, she wanted some explanations.

Built to replace several wooden buildings, the earliest occupants of this two-story brick structure were a saloon and restaurant at 909 Harris Avenue. Next door at 911 Harris, the Cash Grocery, owned by Nels A Anderson and his partner Mr. Lind, was captured in a 1905 photograph. Later the space became Anderson and Halberg Grocery. The second floor was the Bellingham Bay Hotel, with Mrs. Jennie Ruttenbur as the proprietor. The Bacona, a small cigar factory, was also located on the street level at 911, and it is reputed that at one time the Bacona Hotel was also located in 909.

According to the *Fairhaven Gazette*, and historians Penny and Tyrone Tillson, a woman shot herself in the chest in the Bellingham Bay Hotel when her husband abandoned her.

The Investigation

Having looked up the history of the building, I first asked Tina if the smoke smelled like cigars. She was adamant that it didn't. Looking further into the Schering Building next door, I discovered that the original wood Schering had burned down in 1903 and was replaced by more fireproof brick.

That in mind, we began our investigation walking through the dark shop taking pictures for orbs and testing for electromagnetic field (EMF) reactions on our meters. There was activity in odd places, especially in the back room where the visitor center was.

Psychic, Sherry Mulholland, was drawn to the back of the store.

"I felt the presence of a small child. Then I found out that it was the section where they sell baby and children's items."

Although her EMF meter wasn't lighting up, she had "a very strong feeling of energy" which assured her feelings of a child's presence in the building.

Four of us captured photographs of ceiling orbs throughout the store, mostly small ones, but definitely multiplying and moving the longer we stayed. Accompanied by Tina, we settled into the visitor center, where historian Penny Tillson was getting continual red flashes on her EMF meter and psychic Mulholland sat at a table to meditate. She began to sense a strong masculine energy.

Pam Castanera felt the presence also, and described a large, balding man with a belly.

"He has an Alfred Hitchcock look," she said.

Eventually, another man was felt in the room, this one was not as large in stature. Psychics Sherry Mulholland and Pam Castanera began asking questions with their digital recorders on. The rest of us were quiet until I asked that we talk to Tim.

Tim Imus had been the most recent owner of the Bellingham Bay Hotel building, finished the restoration, and then managing it until he passed away of cancer in December of 2010. I had known him well, as he was a Fairhaven fixture. He was a gentle and personable man, popular for his honesty in business and sense of humor, and a good family man. I can't think of anyone who didn't like him.

I had asked his brother Brad, the day before, if we should see if Tim was there, and Brad wondered aloud if that could happen. So, in the building he had once owned, I asked the question.

"Tim, are you here?"

Penny's EMF meter began to spike red in apparent answer. I asked more questions, mentioning some of the things we used to talk about at breakfast in Skylarks when we ran into each other, or how beautiful his home was.

"I loved your chicken coup," I said. "The stained glass was beautiful. You were always very creative."

"Oh?" came the answer by a distinct male voice on the digital recorder. There were no men in our group and no way it could have come from elsewhere without our hearing it. In fact, the response itself seemed shy, almost self-effacing, like Tim would have said it.

After that, he answered no more questions, and the meter quieted down. There was no more activity in that building. We celebrated what we had found, a long lost friend and a few answers to our queries.

Central Hotel. Photo courtesy of Whatcom Museum.

18

The Cowboy Ghost
of the Board of Trade Bar

902 Harris Avenue

At the corner of 9th Street and Harris Avenue, modern Harris Square houses shops and businesses on the street level with luxury bay view condominiums above. Most of its current residents are unaware that restless spirits still occupy a corner shop where a popular bar and hotel once sat.

The Central Hotel was built in 1890 at 902 Harris Avenue, right next door to the brothel district. Mrs. Helga Bullis ran the hotel, her busy rooms just above The Board of Trade Bar. Alexander Berverly was the bar proprietor. (The bar's founder, Thomas Monahan was only there until 1891 before relocating to 11th Street and opening the "New Board of Trade".) Both are pictured below, along with employees in this 1905 photograph.

One hundred and twenty years later at that southeast corner, Southside Trends sells upscale consignment clothing. The store's owner had reported constant problems with the men's shoe section.

"They are always being messed up," said owner, Cathy Lee. "Even if no one has been there looking at them, they are out of order. We've also had display heads fall over for no reason."

Lee also noted that the curtain in the third dressing room was always falling down on its own.

Although the Central Hotel was considered "respectable" in its day, she wondered if perhaps the male borders were searching for their shoes after an evening of "sport" with the ladies. Asked by Lee to check it out, a group of psychics and photographers met there one night in May 2012.

The Investigation

At dusk we arrived with the ghost hunting equipment and the psychics fanned out to the places in the store that drew them the most. Owner, Cathy Lee and employee, Cassie Wolfkill watched nearby. I shot digital photos and immediately captured several orbs floating on a wall where purses hung.

Psychic, Pam Castanera was attracted to the third dressing room mentioned by Cathy, and sat quietly on a bench inside while others began asking questions hoping for EVP recordings.

Right away, sensitive Penny Tillson and psychic Elena Stecca got impressions of a man wearing cowboy boots and a hat. Elena described him as a "worker" type, not a businessman.

While wondering aloud if an entry doorway had once gone through to stairs in the third dressing room, a male voice was recorded by Lena whispering, "the one." She speculated that there was once a door there and the man seemed confused by the current wall. She also noted that he considered himself "very handsome."

Sensitive Tracy Schwent began asking questions, getting strong responses on her EMF detector from the questions, "Do you want to fix the displays in the store?" and "Do you like Cathy?" Since a head mannequin had fallen over by itself that week, Cathy wondered aloud if he had done it.

Then Elena captured a voice.

"At first you can hear Pam's voice very faintly in the background (she was in the small office), then Tracy asked a question. Immediately after the question I heard a male say 'sit down'. I did the echo test to make sure it wasn't a noise and it passed so it is a voice for sure."

In the back of the store in the third dressing room, Pam's EMF meter began beeping loudly. We walked back and stood watching it. The meter sat beside her on the dressing room bench, lighting up to red as it sounded off. There was no one else in the room and no electrical energy to set it off by itself.

I snapped a picture. The flash lit up the dressing room. In an instant, the meter stopped. I apologized to the invisible entity for disrupting it and promised not to take another picture. Eventually, the meter noises began again.

We took a break and gathered around the front counter, where I read a short history of the building. When I mentioned the owners, Alexander and Helga, the meter went wildly to bright red. To make sure it wasn't random, we tried it again. Each time, the EMF meter went red. It also lit up when I mentioned the nearby bordellos and when I asked the group if they wanted to hear more history.

Schwent captured several relevant recordings.

"At 1:07:35 I asked if this was Alexander, there was a pause and then two distinct clicks or taps recorded and at 1:07:39 I asked if this was Helga with us tonight, and the recorder picked up two clicks or taps right after as if in response. I did not hear them at the time but each set is very distinct on the recording."

"At 1:15:54 I was attempting to get a response to 'shave and a haircut' (5 taps) and there was a possible response of two taps or clicks heard on my recorder."

Tracy's report went on to express her disappointment in accidentally erasing an important, and clear EVP.

"Cathy and I had asked for the person we were speaking with to speak louder. The male voice responded, 'louder, louder, louder' very clearly but when I tried to mark the spot on my recorder I erased it instead. This was a voice we did not hear at the time and I am so very disappointed that I cannot share it and must leave it out of the official report."

Later, Pam reported a "real connection" with the man in the dressing room. As she communicated with him telepathically, asking him to set off the meter, the spirit complied each time.

Cassie noted the "warm energy" surrounding the space and sat down on the floor. Pam's notes said, "I felt a real connection with the man in the dressing room. I sat back in the same spot and, these times, I did not ask him out loud to set off the meter, but when I got my brain into the 'zone' again, it kept going off when I silently asked him to. I was amazed. Then Cassie came back and was marveling how peaceful and warm the energy back there felt."

"The meter went off as Cassie sat down on the floor in front of the big dressing room and it was just she and I and whoever the man was. I did indeed feel a male presence, and I have never felt a warm and loving presence, an accepting presence, a supportive presence from a male entity such as this," said Pam.

"We basked in it for awhile, the EMF going off a couple of times. I was picking up that he was 'delighted' by the energy that was coming off of him. Was he delighted with us or with the female attention? I don't know, but it was pure joy to hang with him.

"The others joined us and pretty soon they were all lying on the rug in front of the dressing room, basking, quiet, breathing, like they were on a warm beach on a summer's day. It was quite incredible. Time seemed suspended, and then I didn't feel him anymore, and kind of 'came to' and we all got up and got ready to go."

Shop owner Cathy Lee wrote to me later.

"Amazing evening with so much activity! There seems to be many spirits here. Thank you for making this experience possible. I've never been a skeptic, but my belief is a little stronger now. One thing that did happen is that at at 4:30 in the morning at my home there were two loud knocks in the corner of my bedroom. My husband sat up and looked at the corner. I started laughing and said, 'Now you knock.' The cowboy had finally responded to 'shave and a haircut'."

A couple of weeks later, she reported that the third dressing room curtain was falling repeatedly during the busy Ski to Sea weekend and her staff would put it up over and over again to no avail. She finally went back herself and asked the resident cowboy to stop it. It did not fall again.

The next time I saw Cathy I asked how things were and she was quite comfortable with her spirit visitor. She said he makes noises with the hangars, but she feels he's protective and keeps her company, especially on dark winter evenings.

19

The Brothels of Ninth Street

Ladies of the Evening in long, beautiful dresses have appeared to both psychic investigators and visitors of a number of Fairhaven buildings, including Sycamore Square, Skylarks Café, Harris Square and The Morgan Block. Although they often appear in other buildings, the brothels district lined 9th Street and McKenzie Avenue, and sometimes a walk through the district at night yields voices, orbs and the scent of perfume.

With hundreds of men arriving in Fairhaven daily in the 1890s, smart businesswomen were sure to follow. In search of their own fortunes, women with management skills and the backing to make it happen built brothels large and small, raking in the cash that flowed freely to the workers of this burgeoning seaside town.

There weren't that many options for single women at that time. Unless trained as a teacher or nurse, one was consigned to laundress, cook or nanny. As a high-class prostitute, a woman could make ten times the salary, and enjoy the luxury of the nicer salons. Even women in the "cribs," or small rooms, could earn much more than most other women.

According to historian, Tyrone Tillson, Railroad Avenue, or 9th Street as it is now called, was one of the "meanest streets" in 1890's Fairhaven, the new train tracks leading to dozens of busy brothels, hotels and saloons. "Nice ladies" simply were not seen below 9th or even 10th streets. Eleventh Street was infamously known as "Devil's Row". "Bad ladies" were making a fortune.

As the tracks were laid down 9th street, the workers would walk back into town along the rails for a weekend of gambling and sport with the ladies. Three honest hotels were located there, along with a slew of brothels, the largest of which was Miss Reno's.

A famous "little red book", published in 1891, was a guide to the entertainment not discussed in polite society. Often quoted by historians Tyrone and Penny Tillson, "The Sporting House and Club Directory," ran ads for saloons and cigar stores, along with discreet paragraphs offering the names, address and attractions of those "houses" where the "hostesses" were most accomplished.

The preface read, "The 'Red Book' is intended to be a complete guide to the places of amusement and sport on Bellingham Bay. If there are any omitted it is not our fault. Strangers on the Bay who desire to 'see the sights' will, by referring to its pages be enabled to do so without asking questions."

Specific addresses of brothels include those all the way up to 1410 11th Street, where it is rumored that the upstairs residences held houses of ill repute. At 1009 Larrabee Avenue was Miss Annie Bronson's Palace. 905 Harris had a sporting house on the upper levels in business into the 1940s. (*Fairhaven Gazette*)

Ninth Street, then known as Railroad Ave, was lined mostly with ten-foot wide shacks serving as "Female Boarding Houses". The Bellingham Tennis Club now sits where May B. Wright owned the Castle House. Next door to May's Castle was Cora Beck's House. Kitty corner from the Castle was the elegantly furnished Jewell.

Miss Hattie's on the other hand, was only 12 by 25 feet, squeezed between a plumbing shop, shoe store and meat market. Nearby, the "magnificent and handsome" Misses Arlington and Hill had set themselves apart on a corner lot house both "elegant and genteel". The twenty rooms at Miss Reno's boasted a full staff of "boarders," as referred to in the "Sporting Guide" to Fairhaven's houses of ill repute.

Misses Belle and Lillie ran The Jewell on 9th and McKenzie.

"At The Jewell, it was needless to say that everything is first class and gentility reigns supreme."

Miss Annie's Palace was "a large wooden structure very private and most elegantly furnished. Miss Annie is an extremely experienced hostess, pleasant and agreeable when she entertains her guests. Her boarders are agreeable and polite and of every variety from the saucy little brunette with her glossy curls, to the modest blonde with silken tresses. Here you will always find the gayest and prettiest group in the city."

The Brothels of Bellingham points out that early on, running a brothel was seen as a "legitimate way to earn a living." The 1902 city directory for Whatcom lists Lizzie Rose as a Madam, alongside Mr. C.S. Roray, lumber dealer, and Dr. E.M. Ross, dentist."

Historian, George Hunsby was quoted saying that it was a "tragedy" the brothels were later shut down. "It was good for the town," and a natural thing, he said.

As Tillson wrote, "Stamina did seem to prove a problem with some of the railroad men—in April of 1890 for instance, one unidentified gentleman of the road simply dropped dead while walking down 9th Street."

Some months later, one John Moore, after a rather taxing night at the Gilt Edge Saloon, slept off the evening's entertainment on the new tracks, until the 2:30 train arrived with new revelers. His remains were gathered up the next morning.

O.E. Garland owned a respectable jewelry business on the street, no doubt cleaning up with all the gifting going on between lovesick customers and their ladies. He was a conscientious citizen who served several years as city clerk. He had a hobby of building world-class sailing craft, and unfortunately caught his arm in some lumber mill machinery and it had to be amputated.

Despite the recession of 1893, 9th Street boomed when the city of Whatcom ordered the ladies of leisure out of town and drove them into Fairhaven. The popular May Wright brought her girls to the corner of Ninth and McKenzie to continue the party she started at her large home in earlier years.

A particularly busy place was the Trocadero Dance Hall on Harris Avenue and Seventh Street, a giant hall with curtained second floor box seats from which one could view the dancing below or engage in private activities. Business was so good they excavated the basement to add more rooms, and leased rooms at the nearby Elsemere Hotel.

All was not a party in the early 1900s when the barber at Ninth and Harris admitted to customers that the ringing in his ears had stopped after he had killed his wife and buried her out in the back forty near 30th and Donovan Streets. The police never did find her and mostly didn't want to argue with a guy so good with a razor. (*Fairhaven Gazette*)

Further to the right along 9th street "sat one of the Japanese houses of ill-repute. The proprietor, a Miss Peanut, told the innocent children of the neighborhood they mustn't come visiting when the shades were drawn because that meant that she was already entertaining." (Tyrone Tillson, *Fairhaven Gazette*, Autumn, 1986)

100 years later after the brothel boom, Psychic, Brian Lee worked Graveyard shift while the block-long condominium and retail building, Harris Square, was being constructed between 9th and 10th streets along Harris Avenue. He reported footsteps on empty levels of the building, loud clangs at night and banging noises near where Sirena Gelato now sits.

The ladies of Fairhaven from 100 years ago can appear anywhere in the district and they do. According to psychic Sherry Mulholland, spirits can choose their form when they appear, and it would be natural to want to come back looking youthful and dressed in their finest. If you see a lady in a long, beautiful dress, take a second look to be sure it's someone alive and not a visitor from the past.

The Fairhaven Ladies of the Evening Society at the annual Pacific Northwest Rain Festival. Photo by Leslie Smith.

20

The House on 23rd Street

Happy Valley sits just East of the Fairhaven district. The former farm-
land is now a mixed group of homes from all eras with residents ranging
from college students to families to retirees. Janet lives in an 1889 home
known as the "old Peterson place," to locals who have been here long
enough to know the history. The house has a spirit occupant that is considered part of the family.

Previous to the Peterson's buying it in 1902, the home was built and
occupied by a single woman, Olive Charroin, whose sister lived in the
house next door.

Janet's parents bought the home in 1955. The Peterson's had built it
and lived there up until 1950, until the Smiths bought it, changing the
rooms slightly and adding an upstairs bathroom. Before plumbing, there
had been an outhouse underneath a large lilac tree.

Janet had grown up in the house, so 23 years ago, when it came up for
sale, she and her husband, Rich bought it for their own. But they feel like
they share the house with someone who has been dead a long time.

They call her "Aunt Hilda." She was one of the Petersons, and great
aunt to Fairhaven pharmacist and historian, Gordy Tweit. As Janet grew
up, the family was used to creaking and thumping on the stairs, attribut-
ing it to their resident ghost.

The spirit apparently likes her husband because she has appeared to him twice, standing beside the bed and on the staircase. She wears period clothing and wisps away when he makes eye contact with her.

She's always been in the house. In the 1970s Janet's brother, Erik, remembers hearing loud breathing and snoring, as though someone was sleeping beside him at night. Janet remembers she always had a feeling someone was there looking after her.

"I felt it was a protective spirit," she said. "Especially after the furnace incident."

The furnace had always burned too hot and when the couple bought the house, they replaced it. When it was taken out, the wood boards behind it were severely charred.

"It could have easily caught fire, but for some reason it didn't," she said, adding that perhaps "Aunt Hilda" protected them.

Janet doesn't seem to mind that chairs rock by themselves even when she's sitting in them, and occasionally the bed will be messed up on her husband's side, as though someone slipped under the covers for a little rest.

Once, during a poker game in the garage, a guest saw an apparition cross the room and disappear into the wood stove. Janet's son has discovered orbs floating in pictures he's taken of the living room. Pipe smoke comes and goes through the house. Her father smoked a pipe, and he passed away there.

Still, no one is frightened by the strange comings and goings of the "other" household member.

"We warn friends and family about it," said Janet. "But she's really just family,"

21

The Ghost of Dirty Dan Harris

Entrepreneur, smuggler, curmudgeon, or criminal, Dan Harris left behind a legend. Call him what you will, but he went from a poor East coast whaler to a rich businessman in a few decades. His mark on the frontier town of Fairhaven was unmistakable and unforgettable, but his end was unfortunate. It is said he has never really left Fairhaven and wanders "his town" 100 years later, especially where his "grand" hotel sat at the foot of Harris Avenue and on the Fairhaven Village Green where a bronze likeness now sits.

Harris knew what he wanted for the frontier town he had bought on the bay. He did not name it for himself, or it might have been Dansville or Harrisville. He liked the town of Fairhaven, Massachusetts, and so it became Fairhaven. He wanted straight streets platted and according to an 1891 *Fairhaven Herald*, did not like dead bodies and made the town move the cemetery from "dead man's point" at the foot of Harris Avenue to the corner of 15th Street and Douglas Avenue. No doubt the spirits are still confused.

Harris built the original wood 3-story Fairhaven Hotel in 1883 at the northeast corner of 4th and Harris Avenue near where the Amtrak station now sits, for an astounding $16,000. He then built a mooring dock at the foot of the hotel, charging, it was said, "such outrageous rates that goods have to be unloaded at Bellingham wharf and taken by small boats to Fairhaven."

A bronze statue of Dirty Dan Harris now sits in the Fairhaven
Village Green, and admirers frequently honor and decorate him
with hats, scarves and flowers, and whisper secrets in his ear.
Photo by Taimi Dunn Gorman.

According to Dan Harris historian, Ralph Thacker, *The Reveille*
reported a Mr. James Weed signed a three-year lease on the hotel bringing in furniture in preparation for a building boom and new sawmill on
the bay. It was rated as a good hotel with "best table and beds" and "one
of the best on the sound." A lavish ball and supper took place on June
6th, 1884 with guests reporting elegant style with "lace curtains, walnut
furniture, a piano, and carpets. By 1885 however, Dan was managing the
hotel himself and that same year married Miss Bertha L. Wasmar.

Judge Day was one hotel occupant, and as Justice of the Peace, married couples for two dollars. He had been in the Civil War prior to settling
in the seaside town and ended up owning many Fairhaven businesses.

In 1905, just before Dan's hotel, (by then renamed The Northern
Hotel), was razed to make room for railroad construction, the *Herald*
wrote:

"Lucky, indeed, was the man who had drifted hither with the flood
tide of the boom days to get a bed or a meal at sacrificial prices. There

was no attempt at style. Dan didn›t go much on fin de siecle methods, for he thought all such ‹fol de rol› should be left at the summit of the Rocky Mountains. He aimed to give his guests a wholesome meal and plenty to eat at prices that were in unison with the spirit of the time when a corner lot was worth almost its size in gold and ideals were running high as to the value of dirt....

"The lowest rates at the hotel, even in 1889, were $12.00 a week." (*Fairhaven Gazette*, Autumn, 1987)

Dirty Dan's Sad Demise

Despite his deserved reputation as a clever businessman, "Dirty" Dan Harris ended his days far from his beloved Fairhaven under less than favorable circumstances.

Two years after marrying Bertha Wasmer in 1885, the couple moved to Los Angeles, hoping to improve her failing health with sunshine and warmth. It took several trips back to Fairhaven as he negotiated with Nelson Bennett to purchase the Fairhaven town site, and sadly Bertha passed away and was buried in Los Angeles' Rosedale Cemetery.

Although he had received $70,000 a fortune for 1889, it did not help his grief and he took his one-horse carriage often to the cemetery to lay flowers at her grave. Occasionally, Bertha's former physician, Dr. Shorb, the doctor's wife and his daughter, would accompany him.

The Shorb family took an interest in Dan and his money, with Mrs. Shorb visiting him numerous times a day to comfort him. Dr. Shorb meanwhile, began managing Dan's business dealings and was paid $6,000 for his assistance, the equivalent of twelve years' pay for a common laborer of that time.

Dan also hired a male nurse as he became more bed-ridden from an apparently unexplained illness. The nurse later stated that Dan was "reportedly a bent, strange old man who talked to himself constantly, wore filthy rags in preference to starched underwear, and whose sleeping room was so foul in odor as to attract the attention of any who ventured into the rooms adjoining his abode."

According to Miss Shorb, Dirty Dan Harris was known as "Grease Pot Dan" in Los Angeles. The Shorbs convinced Dan to let the nurse go and they then attended to all of his needs, including administering medicines and offering large daily quantities of whiskey.

He began to give the Shorbs large amounts of money including a Certificate of Deposit worth $25,000. Five weeks later, Daniel Jefferson Harris was dead. The death certificate stated he died of "Pera Carditis," a heart condition. At least, that's what Dr. Shorb told the health officer.

Dan's family was given $45.00 in cash, a pocket watch and household furniture with a total value of $335.

A courtroom battle ensued, and although nephew Benjamin Harris won, he never received any money. It had completely disappeared. Dan was buried under a small, pauper's gravestone beside his wife elaborate tombstone in Los Angeles.

In 1903, just after Fairhaven consolidated with Bellingham, the street department offered a plan to rename all the streets. Harris Avenue was proposed to be renamed "Quincy Avenue". Needless to say, Fairhaven residents put their collective foot down. Local Poet and newspaper editor Frank Tech wrote:

> Don't crowd Dan Harris off the map
> He's crowded off the earth,
> But he really planned that storied street
>   (and gave the town its birth)
> That which was all a work of man and
>   passing fit to wear
> Forever and a day the name of the man
>   who fixed it there.
> Don't push poor Harris out of our town
>   your scheme is out of joint
> It doesn't include the historic tag
>   and bow to a dead man's point...

(Fairhaven Gazette, Autumn 1992, Penny and Ty Tillson, historians)

22

The Haunted Hotel

The Fairhaven Hotel
1890 – 1953

The ornate Fairhaven Hotel was considered the crown of the boom-town on the bay. The one-block-square grand palace was built with the $300,000 investment of local businessman, C.X. Larrabee, hoping to cash in when the railroad terminus came. The rich adored it. Mark Twain stayed there. Unfortunately, it was also the location of his meeting with railroad financier, Jim Hill, who broke the news that the railroad would go to Seattle, not Fairhaven.

As a hotel, it never paid for itself, though it stood as a monument to what could have been. Locals held grand balls over the years and it was considered the finest accommodation around. The Larrabee family lived there, and their daughter, Mary Adele, one of four children, was born there in 1903. They stayed in the hotel until building their mansion, Lairmont Manor.

Unfortunately, C.X never lived in his opulent new manor house. One day after conducting his usual business looking over his Samish oyster flats, he took the interurban train back to the hotel. Just before entering the Harris Avenue vestibule, he collapsed and was carried inside by his friend Cyrus Gates. He regained consciousness long enough to say, "I'm all right!" and then he died.

The opulent Fairhaven Hotel across from the Mason Block at 12th Street and Harris Avenue, it burned in 1953.

Final services were held in the dining room of the hotel on September 18th, 1914. The family moved soon after. Then the hotel remained empty for a while.

In 1922, according to historian George Hunsby, it became the location of a yogurt manufacturer and eventually another group purchased it as a hotel, renaming it "The Victorian Hotel." It didn't succeed and the edifice stood vacant again.

After years it became the Whatcom Welfare Office and then the Fairhaven Lions Club installed a popular Boy's Club, which moved and evolved into what is now the successful Whatcom Boys & Girl's Club." The Lions Club held social events there and kept the building alive.

The last owner was a local florist. Then, in 1953 it burned in a spectacular fire and the property sold for a mere $2500. What was left of the grand castle was used as shoreline fill in the marshlands near 6th and Harris Avenue.

It is said that the spirits from that grand hotel still hold their balls and formal social gatherings across the street at Sycamore Square, Fairhaven's ghost central. The lot where the hotel sat, featured colorful old train cars housing small shops and cafes for a while, but has held only a vacant service station and small strip mall for many years. Occasionally an investor talks of resurrecting the building, but like the spirits who visit, nothing has yet materialized.

23

The Lady of the Waldron

The Waldron Building
12th Street & McKenzie Avenue
Built 1891

One of the grandest buildings in Fairhaven still dominates the corner of 12th Street and McKenzie Avenue with huge stones and an elegantly rounded corner. Though now occupied by upscale tenants in million dollar condos, if you look carefully, one might see a transparent face in a window, or feel a chill while walking by at dusk. Reports of supernatural residents still trickle in from those who spend time there.

The Waldron was built in 1891, by Fairhaven's first banker, Charles Waldron, of ballast bricks from Japanese sailing ships. He had arrived from Michigan in 1889, and by the spring of 1890, owned more property than anyone else in the area.

Unfortunately, the bank closed in spring of 1894 after Mr. Waldron was arrested for not honoring customer checks. After a "few days in Fairhaven's calaboose at 1112 Donovan—and possible talk of a lynching…" (*Fairhaven Gazette*), Mr. Waldron saw the error of his ways.

Adding to his difficulties had been a disastrous fire, which had gutted the northern half of the building in January, closing the Cissna Department store at 1308–1310 12th Street. Even with approximately a half-acre of floor space, only the first two floors were ever used. It went bust before filling up.

The second floor served both as a hotel and commercial house, for such businesses as Painless Sims Dental surgery, and Vincent Cole, coronet player. Charles Waldron lived next to the Card Room.

After the fire, George Hohl opened a feed and seed store where the department store had been.

After prohibition and the depression of the 1930s, the Kulshan Tavern was located on the corner with Ed's Tavern (named The Fairhaven in the 1970s) nearby in the northern half of the building. Both dominated the building and partied hard for over thirty years, along with "Crazy" Richard's Soup and Sandwich Gallery. The taverns became hippie icons in the late 1960s and early '70s, legendary for their drug and booze fueled nights and their shabby condition.

The buildings were derelict. Penny Tillson talked of having to walk on a wood plank over mud to get to the ladies room. Artist, George Jartos broke his foot in a hole in the floor while dancing at the Kulshan.

Jartos said that the harassment of hippies became the norm by the local police, trying to crack down on the drug usage and partying in the district. Hired to paint the ceiling mural at The Fairhaven, Jartos was nearly busted for drinking beer on election day.

Apparently all bars were closed for elections, apparently to prevent either drunken voting or beer bribes. The owner of the bar was doing the books while drinking apple juice from a schooner when the police came in to sniff around. Not finding the beer they'd hoped for in her glass, they fortunately didn't notice Jartos' coffee cup.

Purchased in the 1970s by the Imus family, the taverns were gone from the Waldron by 1974. The Fairhaven moved into Finnegan's Alley and the building remained mostly boarded up at street level, with the empty upper floors eventually receiving windows as it waited decades for restoration. In 2006, the building was extensively renovated by developer, David Ebenal, with a bank in the corner once again, and luxury view condominiums on the upper floors. Six years later we got a report of spirit activity from tenants.

Restoration of the Waldron Building.
Photo by Taimi Dunn Gorman

A business located in the Waldron in the year 2012 contacted psychics with a complaint of occasional rotting smells and strange and frightening sensations in the back hallways by the restroom. We went in one night to have a look.

The Investigation

We met in the business conference room, sitting with lights off as darkness fell outside and courtyard lights came on. Psychics, Chuck Crooks and Brian Lee, took EMF meter readings around the room and hallway, but picked up no activity. Sherry Mulholland sat asking Carla Lee what her experiences had been in the space.

I walked around the table taking pictures of the walls, ceiling and floor, and immediately began to get tiny orbs, especially all over the north wall. After talking the guys stood up again and went back into the hall. Brian sensed coolness "like rainwater" up to his knees. Chuck stepped into a closet and felt the sensation of cobwebs on his head. Brian said later that the feeling of spider or cobwebs when nothing was present was sometimes a sign of passing through the "veil" from this world to the next.

A strong female energy began to come to Chuck, but when Brian got closer, it would pull back. Sherry took a chair into the hallway by the restroom and turned on the water in the sink in hopes of giving the spirit kinetic energy to manifest itself.

"A young woman between the ages of 20 to 25 presented herself, happy and upbeat and wanting to let us know she was there," said Mulholland. "She dressed in bright colors and wanted me to know that she served men in a 'gentlemanly' way. She made it quite clear she prefers men of white color and professional status and enjoyed meeting them at their offices. I was able to see her, but that's all."

"She communicated to me by giving me images of her and part of her story. I was completely fascinated by her. When I joined the rest of our party around the conference table, she seemed to join us and stayed peculiarly close to Chuck. From this point on it was about teasing and flirting with Chuck. Her attraction was most evident in that she completely ignored the rest of our group."

The three sensed that the "lady of the evening" came from the late 1800s. She wore light colored clothing and liked flowers. She also liked well-dressed men, especially men in suits. It appeared that since Chuck was the better dressed of the two men, she liked him a lot. She kept showing Sherry a visualization of a man at a desk that she liked to visit.

After talking to Carla and realizing that the present business had all female employees, we realized that this vision must have been from the original Bank of Fairhaven, located at that corner, which would have employed only men.

Sitting back together in the conference room, Chuck put some money on the table and asked the "lady" to interact with him. I shot pictures as orbs floated above and next to him, especially beside his ear. He sensed her blowing in his ear and touching his hair. It was enthralling to watch and affirmed repeatedly by the photographs.

Meanwhile, Brian got a sense of a man nearby in a chocolate brown suit. He said his last name was Taylor and he seemed to be troubled that his watch was missing. It didn't appear that the "lady" was interacting with Taylor.

As we left, we each reminded the spirits that they needed to stay in the Waldron Building and not come home with us. Chuck was very adamant about this with the "lady," especially since he'd had a negative entity go home with him once and pounded on a wall all night trying to get his attention. He didn't need a repeat performance. We left promising to return again to visit the ghosts of the Waldron.

Epilogue

Curious about the unusually small size of the orbs we encountered at the Waldron Building, I did some research on orb photography and discovered that the new Nikon camera I had just purchased contained an infrared filter, diminishing the number and size of orbs that appear. I've since returned to an older Coolpix sans filter.

Also, the Lady of the Evening continued to visit Chuck for weeks afterward, appearing in his dreams trying to seduce him, and even returning during investigations of other Fairhaven buildings. One morning he awoke to find that after thinking he heard his roommate shower and whistle a tune, she wasn't even at home. The Lady may still be stalking him.

24

Spirit Central

The Fairhaven Library

1117 12th St
Circa 1904

Until we visited the Fairhaven Library, I had assumed Sycamore Square was the "most haunted" building in the Historic Fairhaven district. After all, it's the one visited by all the ghost hunters, there are photos of the spirits on their website, and everyone talks about its supernatural occupants as though it's a natural thing. After a night in the Library having one of the scariest investigations I'd ever been on, the honor of "Fairhaven's most haunted" has been bestowed on the outwardly sedate library.

For some reason, perhaps because no one ever reported any paranormal activity, the 108-year-old building was never listed in the Fairhaven Haunted Brochure, and it had not been investigated by any of the psychics in our group. We were curious, but at the same time, we didn't expect a big night of spirit interaction there. I was shocked by the end of the night.

One psychic, Pam Castanera, described in her report how I looked.

"Poor Taimi was a wreck almost the whole time, by the end of the night she had no make up on, her eyes were bloodshot, and she looked like she'd been through a huge storm."

In fact, I felt like I'd been through a storm of paranormal activity like I'd never imagined.

Donna Grasdock, a Library Specialist who is in charge of the library's community rooms, was curious enough about the history of the place to invite us in late one night for a look.

The two-story brick structure with a basement was financed with a grant from industrialist, Andrew Carnegie, who funded numerous libraries around the country. Fairhaven citizens were anxious to have a space "for men to spend their evenings besides in the saloons."

Originally opened in the Fairhaven Bank Building, the library moved into the Mason Block (Sycamore Square) in 1891, only to get its own home in December, of 1904. Local businessman, C.X Larrabee and his wife donated the two vacant lots. His portrait still sits in the basement Fireplace Room.

To the right beneath the main concrete stairs into the library is a second entrance leading to the basement rooms. There was a separate reading room located there for men in their working clothes, so the scent of fish, body odor and other manly fragrances didn't offend the olfactory glands of genteel ladies. The basement was also home to a children's area, restrooms and the heating plant.

The library and reading room was on the main floor, with a large, wood floor meeting and performance space on the top level.

Despite the neighborhood popularity of the library, it hadn't been well built, and the loose bricks and stucco deteriorated in the damp climate. By 1970, a bond measure to demolish it and build a new one failed, so a minor, and unfortunately not in period, remodel took place instead. After being placed on the National Register of Historic Places in 1977, the next remodels were more sensitive to the fine glass and woodwork in the building.

The Investigation

Donna, the librarian had told us that the main source of paranormal complaints came about the basement conference rooms, but we began with a short meeting in the comfortable main floor chairs. Immediately, orbs began to appear. By the end of the night we had dozens of photographs. (Find several on www.hauntedfairhaven.com.)

Transparent orb floating in front of a portrait of C.X. Larrabee,
in the Fireplace Room of the Fairhaven Library.
Photo by Leslie Smith.

Having walked the main library, we moved into the children's area, now located in a room toward the back of that floor. Our electromagnetic field meters began going off immediately in areas where there was no obvious wiring. They flashed red at a rocking chair and stopped when we removed the stuffed animals on it. They flashed by the books, the toys and the table.

Psychics Pam Castanera and Elena Stecca, sensed a young boy who seemed to be quite happy to be in the library, as though it were his home. When asked questions, he happily replied "yup" on the digital recorder. Another recording, which may have been from the same boy, said "thank you."

We photographed dozens of orbs, some floating at low levels near the floor, and more near the ceiling interacting as though they were children playing together.

Then Donna escorted us down a back staircase to the basement conference rooms. There are spaces downstairs, the largest of which is the "Fireplace Room." This was the original reading room for working men in Fairhaven. We gathered in a circle on the carpeted floor to see if anything would come out for us in the dark.

Photographer, Leslie Smith sat nearby, taking pictures. Her repeated "oh, my God" exclamations made me move in closer to the others, as she reported we were surrounded on the floor by orbs. She captured a large one right in front of the portrait of C.X. Larrabee.

I shot photos as well, and discovered that the orbs seemed to move in groups, like a flock of birds. There were so many, we felt nearly knee deep at times as it appeared in the pictures we were taking. They moved fast, not slow as dust particles might, and ranged in size from tiny to at least a foot in width. Every time we shot a picture they had moved.

In the meeting room across the hall, Pam picked up a psychic message from someone saying that they "missed the balloons at the large birthday parties" they used to throw. The librarian confirmed that they had indeed stopped hosting annual parties for the library, but figured if the ghosts missed them maybe it was time to bring them back.

As we walked up the staircase to the top level, several unsettling things occurred. Both Elena and Pam felt as though a man was following us, though keeping his distance.

"I occasionally could hear him shouting something at us but he was too far to tell what he was saying," said Elena afterward.

The shouting and anger followed us upstairs and even I heard him as we stepped into the wood floored ballroom on the top floor. In addition, the orbs had gathered along the stairs and up the walls, with every picture we took revealing more of them.

At the top of the stairs was a ticket window for the ballroom and it felt almost as though the orbs were lined up as customers for the show.

Electromagnetic Field detectors went red all over the room, especially on the piano bench and beside the piano. If an invisible concert was going on, the orbs were in attendance, also. One appeared on Elena's stomach and more were around the room. A large one floated beside the wood paneled windows.

Back on the main floor, we asked Donna, the librarian, if there were any places she felt uncomfortable going. She took us to a downstairs storeroom beside a back staircase and said she always had a strange feeling there. I took a picture and got half an orb on the stairs, as though it were trying to hide. Pam recoiled back from the steps as though someone had hit her.

"I can't go up there," she said suddenly. "There is a really angry male energy there." She closed her eyes and shook her head as though to clear him away.

She reported later that she became enraged at the entity and the anger he generated toward her. "I just wanted to hit something," said Pam.

As the negative energy dissipated, we cautiously walked up the stairs to the main level and prepared to leave. After gathering our equipment and thanking Donna, Pam and then Elena, stated aloud and firmly, "nothing is going home with us." I seconded that and we went off into the night.

" YOU DON'T BELIEVE THAT STUFF ABOUT CLASSROOM 313 BEING HAUNTED DO YOU?

Cartoon courtesy of George Jartos.

25

The Tragedies
of the Monahan Building

1209 11th Street
Built 1890

There have been reports through the years of strange occurrences on the upper floor of the Monahan Building, which once served as residences, but for the past few decades have housed various health care practitioners, massage therapists and counselors. Several tenants have told me about a feeling of being watched and discomfort in the hallway.

Workers and the owner of the retail shop on the main floor have not had such experiences, and owners of the building since 2000 said they've had nothing happen, but it wouldn't be surprising considering the tragic history of the building.

The Turf Saloon, owned by Thomas Monahan and operated by his sons, was the first tenant on the street level selling liquor and good wines, and offering gambling. It was reputed to be a respectable business, unlike many in Fairhaven at the time.

He later changed the name to "The New Board of Trade" saloon (after his first Irish Saloon on Harris Avenue), selling less expensive booze to keep up with the economic times. The Monahan family lived upstairs.

It was reported that Tom Monahan loved fast horses and one evening was thrown from his buggy on 10th street, landing on his head. It was said his wife died of a broken heart and was laid beside him shortly after.

After the town went dry in 1920, entrepreneur, George Finnegan, ran the Fairhaven Pharmacy there for a while, and in 1949, John Sandwick, the son of Otto Sandwick, a confectioner, moved Sandwick's Grocery and Fountain onto the main floor after being dislocated by a fire. The family, including Otto's widow, Olga, lived upstairs through the 1950s.

Historian, Gordy Tweit fondly remembers the marble counter and the shop's delicious fudge. Gordy also remembers something else more unfortunate.

"The Sandwick boy had been handicapped after the brakes gave out on his bike and he hit a car and landed on his head," said Gordy. "When he was older, he died of natural causes in one of the upstairs apartments and they didn't find him for days. Everyone thought he was in Skagit (County) visiting his cousins.

"The older Sandwick got to be an alcoholic toward the end. He would go out and drink a lot and borrow money."

The Monahan Saloon, Thomas E. Monahan, proprietor, 1905.
Courtesy of Whatcom Museum.

The Investigation

Hoping to connect with whatever spirits may still linger in the building I contacted Steve Roguski, owner of the Fairhaven Runners and Walkers store on the 11th street main floor. He allowed us access to both the shop and the upstairs hallway.

Psychics Sherry Mulholland, Pam Castanera and Chuck Crooks joined me in the investigation. Once the staff had closed for the evening, we walked through the shop with our EMF meters and recorders. I took several photos looking for orbs, but had no luck.

I was astonished by something in the rear of the building. The public does not get to see the back door, which is shielded from view by a wooden storage structure. Enormous, fortress-like metal door and window covers now hang unused on the brick wall. It was obvious that at one time they had something precious to protect in this space. Very likely, it was Mr. Monahan's liquor store.

We then split up, with Sherry remaining in the shoe store and Pam, Chuck and I going upstairs to where the offices, (formerly apartments) open into a hallway. Since the offices were all closed for the night, we walked the hall with our EMF meters and cameras and I began to get orb photos.

The pictures weren't as impressive as some we've seen and we made no direct contact with any spirits, but oddly, Chuck began to sense the Lady of the Evening who continued to follow him since the visit to the Waldron Building. We asked if Mr. Sandwick was present or if Mr. Monahan was there, but got no response.

Having spent enough time getting bad orb pictures, I went downstairs to see what Sherry was doing. I set my EMF meter on the bench beside me and she began to sense a male presence joining us. I asked if it was Thomas Monahan. The meter began to blink red.

What followed was a long conversation with a ghost. The first I'd really had in the investigations. I asked him if he enjoyed making money, if he liked his store and if he was proud of his horses. Each time the meter blinked red for me.

When I asked if he had ever visited the brothels, he did not respond, but when we asked his wife's name and gave him letters to choose from, he blinked at K.

"Was her name Kate?" I asked. The meter blinked again. I could not find any history on her later, so I can't say if it was true or not.

By the time we were joined by the others, the meter blinking had slowed considerably and we reasoned that both our ghost and ourselves had run out of steam. We left happy that we'd made contact with the resident spirit and that he seemed quite content visiting his old liquor establishment.

If you're walking down 11th Street some quiet night, look up at the Monahan Building and see if anything, or anyone, is looking back at you. Restless spirits who once resided there still remain for those who can see them.

Pythias Building. Photo courtesy of Whatcom Museum.

26

The Secret Societies of The Pythias Building

1204 – 1210 11th St
Built 1891

While awaiting a new location being built for them at the corner of
Harris and 11th Streets in May of 2012, Fairhaven's popular garden shop,
A Lot of Flowers, moved into a basement space in the Pythias Building
beside my former restaurant, the Colophon Café. The shop was cheerful,
painted in bright colors, with flowers, painted pots and garden items for
sale.

I dropped in one day to say hello and employee Kelly Swordmaker
asked if the ghost investigation group would come in and figure out what
was going on. Since they had moved in, they'd seen shadow figures, had
strange feelings of someone being there, and worst of all, customers were
dropping in and leaving quickly without explanation.

The energy was heavy in the space, despite the colorful merchandise,
fragrant scents and beautiful live plants. I moved around with my EMF
meter and got strong readings in two places pointed out by Kelly and her
sister, shop owner, Penny Ferguson. I promised we'd come on Sunday
night when things were quiet.

The Pythias Building is one of the tallest and most mysterious looking of the 1890's brick buildings erected during Fairhaven's boom. Originally built to house the "secret societies" of Fairhaven, it has held dozens of businesses over its long history.

A basement sits below 11th street, opening out to what is now the Fairhaven Village Green. The 11th Street main level has been home to the Colophon Café since 1985, and Pacific Chef sits next door where Village Books was located until they build a new home two doors down several years ago.

The top two floors have been vacant and the windows mostly boarded up for many years. When I co-owned the Colophon Café, from 1985 to 2002, I had a key to those floors. Once, when I was exploring the ancient wood-floored apartments on the second floor, I found a yellowed newspaper dated from the 1940s, although I'd heard tales that in the 1960s and '70s before the Imus family bought it, hippies lived there, entering through the fire escape on the back wall even though the building had been deemed uninhabitable at least a decade earlier.

In my visits, the original tattered wallpaper was still on the walls. Ornate wood doorways and bannisters and the high ceilings were traditional to the era. A staircase in the center of the building opened to a view of a now dirty and leaky glass skylight in the center of the roof.

The top floor was a gem frozen in time. Two enormous ballrooms where the secret societies of Fairhaven once met, took up the entire floor. The smaller room, used by the Masons, overlooked 11th street and had a peephole in the door to monitor entrance to what was later a speakeasy.

Spaciously overlooking the Fairhaven Village Green and the entirety of Bellingham Bay, the large ballroom, known as "Castle Hall", had a high ceiling, wood floors, brick walls, and a small stage. It had been home to meetings and gatherings of the Pythias Society. The huge windows were always breaking during winter storms in the 1980s and '90s due to their age. Dead birds lay about and were a constant problem for the Imus family, who owned the building at that time and tried to keep it maintained.

Visiting the ballrooms or the second floor apartments, with bathtubs, and other fixtures still intact, always made my hair stand up. I felt as though I was not alone on those visits, and in fact, never went up there without lots of company with me. It was an annual trip we allowed the

café staff to go upstairs and explore so they could answer curious customers when they asked about the strange, vacant floors.

The main floor and basement had housed numerous businesses over
the building's 100-plus years, including a hardware store, kitchen shop, an
ice cream parlor and even a car repair garage in the basement. Whatcom
Museum historian, Jeff Jewell wrote that embalmer and coroner, John M.
Warriner moved his funeral parlor from 14th street to the Pythias Building
in the late 1890s until it was sold and moved to downtown Bellingham
in 1903. (Warriner had also been the one responsible for the removal of
bones from Deadman's Point, relocating them to Bayview Cemetery.)

In June of 1985, Ray Dunn and I opened the Colophon Café at 1208
11th Street, beside Village Books at the time. The building was mostly
otherwise vacant, with nothing but storage in the basement and empty
rooms on the top two floors. Eventually, both the busy bookstore and the
Colophon expanded into the basement. Building owner Ken Imus built a
staircase and installed windows and lighting to cheer up the former car
repair space. An entry was cut through the wall into an author reading
room beneath Paper Dreams.

In the early 1990s, Ray was sitting in the basement office under the
stairs working at about 4 a.m., when he heard distinct footsteps on the
wood floor at the 11th Street level. He crept up the stairs in the inky
blackness, expecting to find someone walking around. There was no one
in sight. He was alone in the building.

A former Colophon employee claimed to have seen an apparition of a
woman standing inside the downstairs restroom, and another said that the
upstairs restroom was just "creepy", with strange noises, every time she
went in to change for work.

The recurring noises disappeared in later years as the café bakery
began all-night shifts with rock music. It was assumed that the restless
spirits moved to the higher, quieter floors.

Village Books built a new building on the corner of 11th and Mill
Avenue, and Pacific Chef opened in the 11th Street space beside the
Colophon. When she heard I was writing this book, former Pacific Chef
employee, Cassie Wolfkill, told me that a customer had come in one day,
walked around, said she was a psychic and "it was a powerful place".

"As she left the store, a huge gust of wind came through and knocked everything off the front table," said Cassie, still remembering the shock of the incident.

Other staff had reported kitchen utensils flying off the walls and one day a large vase suddenly exploded by the front window.

So apparently the ghosts hadn't left. In June 2012, while awaiting their new building, A Lot of Flowers was experiencing supernatural disturbances and it was time for us to visit.

The investigation

Kelly Swordmaker greeted us at A Lot of Flowers for our investigation. It was getting dark outside and we kept the lights off in the shop, seeing with the ambient light from the Colophon next door. Our EMF meter lights were easy to see in the dark and they once again began to go off in the back of the shop and in the center display area.

Kelly told us that a psychic had dropped in the other day and told her they had three spirits in the store. She said she contacted each and asked them to leave. I was hoping they'd actually left so we wouldn't have to deal with them.

Perhaps they had, I thought as we began walking around. I was tripping over plants in the dark. Although the meters went off several times, psychics Chuck Crooks and Elena Stecca found only one angry spirit in the back storage room where customers don't go. They left him alone.

Their colleague, Brian Lee was broadcasting our investigation live on his Barncat radio show and we took turns reporting on air what we were finding. The thirty-minute recording ended up covering the basics of our investigations throughout Fairhaven and the upcoming book that would result.

In the next room, Psychic Pam Castanera had settled into a booth near the Colophon's kitchen, joined by historian, Penny Tillson, who had her EMF meter on.

"This building has lots of sandstone brick walls," said Castanera, "and I felt compelled to put my hands flat on the wall. There was a slight vibration, but, as it has before with old buildings, caused pictures to flash in my head."

"All the pictures that came to me were scenes of Native Americans, dressed in skins and feathers, (not appearing ceremonial) outside, doing chores, cooking over a fire, lots of kids around. Just like a normal day in their lives. I can say, with all honesty, I have never before had pictures of Native Americans in my head, like that. Almost like a tableau."

She continued, "So I told Penny what I was sensing, and she said that indeed they had lived around Fairhaven in large groups in the 1700-1800s and smaller communities dating back to 800 B.C."

In fact Fairhaven locals know 10th Street as an old Indian trail and currently part of the waterfront public trail system to Boulevard Park.

Lummi canoes in Fairhaven. Photo courtesy of Whatcom Museum.

They sat together in the booth with Castanera's digital voice recorder and Tillson's EMF meter, which was beginning to go to red, showing electromagnetic spirit activity beside them.

"So I started talking," said Castanera, "Encouraging whoever it was (I felt male energy) that was listening to our conversation on local history, to make the EMF blink really fast, and instructed him on how to do it."

"The EMF meter went crazy on and off for what seemed like a long time. Then off for 5 minutes or so, then back on with a fury. This continued for some time to our amazement. No voices were recorded due to the background music in the kitchen, so we moved toward the glass outside doors facing the Village Green."

"The spirit followed us, as requested, but as we got to the booth, he was with us and then was gone," said Castanera.

Seeing that the spirit activity had finally ceased for Pam, I called a short meeting with everyone to share the history of the building, including when it was built, the various businesses that had been there and the ongoing reports of activity in the space where Pacific Chef now resides. We speculated that the funeral parlor had occupied that space because a hardware store had been in the Colophon Café at that time. Then we went upstairs to the Colophon diner area.

"As the group packed up," said Castanera, "I went up the stairs first. Inexplicably, I immediately took a sharp left turn at the top of the stairs. It was a hallway leading to locked doors going into the Paper Dreams shop. I stood there for a minute getting my bearings and I immediately felt the strong presence of an angry male spirit."

"I wanted to turn and leave. But I stayed and kept feeling this energy upon me. My body reacted like it always does with nausea, but I also felt a clenched, anxious feeling in my chest that I have never felt before."

"Chuck (Crooks) came up and I told him what I was feeling, and went to go sit in a booth to calm down. My heart was racing," said Castanera.

Neither Chuck or Brian felt it, but I sat with Pam in the booth getting the familiar nausea I get also when a spirit is very close. Everyone else was up there by then investigating the entryway. Pam decided to go back and see what would happen.

"The feelings returned with a vengeance," said Castanera, shuddering at the memory.

"I got goose bumps which wouldn't go away, and the nausea and anxiety came back. I held out my recorder to ask a question and as soon as I did that I had this overwhelming sensation of fear for my safety, as I felt he was going to knock the recorder out of my hand or hit me. The anger was palpable and thick."

"I said to Penny, who was standing beside me, 'I have to leave, I'm afraid he's going to hit me', and I quickly retreated to the booth with Taimi, who was taking pictures of the group from the booth with her cell phone. (She had forgotten her equipment box that night.) I have never, in all my investigations, felt a negative energy as strong as his," said Castanera.

Exhausted by our communications with whatever entities were occupying the Pythias Building, we called it a night and went home.

While loading my cell phone pictures later that night, I was stunned to see I had captured a large speeding orb headed straight for Elena's chest. She had been sitting in one of the chairs in the hallway. (Unfortunately, the photo was taken in the dark and is too fuzzy to print, but you can find it at www.hauntedfairhaven.com). Elena also experienced the negativity that emanated from the spot. It seemed only the guys were immune.

When I dropped into A Lot of Flowers the next day, Kelly and Penny told me they'd just had the biggest sales day they'd had since moving into the space.

27

Orb Central

The Schering Block
Also known by long-time South-siders as the Jenkins-Boys Building
913 – 915 Harris Avenue
Built 1903

The Schering Block is a quiet, commercial building where most tenants stay a long time and there are few reports of unusual activities. Archer Ale House occupies the basement, Renaissance Celebration glass shop dominates the corner space with The Chimney Sweep to its left, and The Blue Moon Salon sits by the front entrance on 10th Street. Massage therapists and counselors keep their practice in the upstairs offices. A tip from a shop employee sent the ghost investigators in for a look around.

Owner, Brad Imus, and his wife, Jean, who began work on the building in 1978, took years to renovate and improve this now pleasant brick structure, even having lived in it for a time. As with most Fairhaven edifices, The Schering Block has a long history of ghost-creating activity over the years, including housing a busy saloon, pioneer courthouse, a social hall and a hippie commune.

Charles Schering bought this empty lot in 1883 from his brother-in-law property mogul, Dirty Dan Harris, and built a one-story wooden building here. It was home to the Elk Saloon and Café until an unfor-

tunate 3:00 am fire consumed the entire structure on January 31, 1903.
Schering was insured and quickly rebuilt a grander a two-story building
for $10,000.

The busy Elk Saloon returned to its former location and in 1905. The
owners were John Mack and F. R. Abeel.

The Elk Bar with the bartender Fred Liebman in front.
Photo courtesy of Whatcom Museum.

People were not the only patrons of the infamous Elk Bar. Meat sup-
plier Joe Alsop met ships on the dock every Thursday for the latest ship-
ment of cows, sheep and hogs; and rather than negotiate the tricky turn
onto 10th Street, the cattle would stumble into the Elk Saloon or other
nearby businesses, creating a scene out of the movie "Blazing Saddles".

The second floor housed a large wood-floored hall, which in 1909
seated 50 in Peace Judge Henry C. Beach's courthouse. Dr. Brier also saw
patients in an upper floor office. The retail space at 913 Harris beside the
Elk was occupied from 1903 to 1916 by a hardware store, owned by Jacob
and Harry C. Jenkins and Fred Boys. Around the corner at 1208 10th
Street was a printing business.

The Dry Ballot of 1910 forced the closure of all drinking establishments, vacating the Elk saloon. Seeing a good opportunity, businessman and pharmacist, George Finnegan opened a cigar store in the prominent corner space.

By the 1930s, the top floor meeting space was opened up and became the Croatian Hall, used for lively social dances and celebrations by the large Fairhaven Slavic community of fishermen and their families. After the 1940s it closed down and a fiberglass boat-building firm, Wright Manufacturing Company, using a crane to lower them from the top floor when they were finished.

By the late 1960s, the top floor had been vacated and hippies moved in to create a commune during Fairhaven's 'free love' days.

In 1972, Ken Imus of Jacaranda Development Company purchased the Schering Block and began renovations, finished by his son, Brad. Although Brad hasn't had any odd experiences in the building, and in fact, his office is in there. He was open to our "spirit safari" on June 1st, 2012.

The Investigation

Two psychics, a photographer, our historian and myself ventured into the upstairs hallway of the Schering building, frankly not knowing what to expect. I had assumed there wouldn't be a lot going on. After all, my PR office used to be up there and I felt a lot more comfortable there than I ever did in the Doggie Diner on Harris Avenue. But quiet and sedate, it was not to be. As psychic, Sherry Mulholland said later,

"There was a lot more energy than I had expected."

Drawn to sit on a couch near the restrooms, she captured an EVP recording that didn't make sense. "Big swag", it said. But it wasn't long before a reading came through that everyone recognized. "Bitch", a woman exclaimed.

Penny Tillson, Leslie Smith and I all began taking photographs, with Leslie getting some of the largest white orbs we had seen. There were groups of orbs around the hallway, on the couch, the floor and beside the windows of the back offices. They moved around us and changed position with our shots.

A particularly large orb floats outside an office door at the
Schering Building. Photo by Leslie Smith.

Mulholland continued, "Once I settled comfortably on the couch the first name of Andy came to me along with an image of Aunt Jemima from the pancake mix."

Along with this odd pairing, a last name of Blake or Blakely was presented to her. When she told me this later, I pointed out that the courthouse had been in the building and perhaps Marshal Blakely, who also lived in Sycamore Square, was trying to contact her.

"Afterwards", she said, "I felt the presence of a woman about the size of our author (Taimi). She may have passed while in her fifties. She didn't pass with a sudden death. It was more prolonged. She was able to say goodbye to family and loved ones. The names of Lilly, Lilith, Elizabeth, perhaps Liz were given to me. She was trying to present herself as younger than when she passed. She was more comfortable with her younger age."

By the time we finished it was 11:30 p.m., and we were famished from the scent of cooking drifting up from the Archer Ale House in the basement. Although a half hour before closing, the waitress put in our order for the baked cheesy "Irish Nacho" potatoes, which take over 20 minutes to make. I couldn't help but turn on my EMF detector to see what was around us.

The Archer is a British-style pub with lots of European character. A great selection of beers and a respectable wine list compliment their homemade munchies and sandwiches. The dart boards in the back are nearly always occupied with contestants. Old photographs, art prints and beer art and mirrors line the mostly brick and old stone walls.

When we finished eating we confessed to the waitress that we would like to stay and investigate the bar, and she complied. Sherry chose a table to "ground" herself and asked to talk to the spirit of the owner who had passed away last year.

She then recorded a very clear class A EVP of the words "quack quack".

"Was he wanting to mimic a duck or were we being called Quacks?" mused Sherry. "I don't think we'll ever know for sure."

We captured numerous orb photos in the back of the pub where the dartboards are. This intrigued us so much that we made an appointment with the owners to come back another night and try again.

Large orb floating in the Archer Ale House. Photo by Leslie Smith.

Our second visit was much less sedate. A Coast Guard vessel was in dry dock, and a large group of Coast Guardsmen were packed in the Pub partying and weren't in the mood to go home. We set up our equipment and began taking pictures and measuring for EMF activity anyway, with the curious sailors asking questions about ghosts. With the noise it was impossible to get any voice recordings.

There were orbs though, lots of them. They showed up in several photographs, along with an extremely strange light that appeared on one of the men as he left the bar. The owner's wife, Alicia, and an employee posed for a photograph and I could not explain the light that shows up. If it's a reflection, what was it reflecting off of?

An odd light shows up on the jacket of a patron leaving the Archer Ale House (left). Photo by Taimi Dunn Gorman.

The psychics stayed late, hoping to get some EVP recordings, but it wasn't to be. Eventually, they called it a night and went home. The Archer Ale House in the basement of the Schering Building appears to have more visitors than just the patrons. It seems to be crowded apparently even when no one is there.

28

The Waiting Lady

The ghost tale Lauren Taylor shared with me over red wine at Skylarks one day was chilling. As one of the dozen characters in the Historic Fairhaven "Ladies of the Evening Society," we've spent a lot of time together over the years in 1890's madam costumes entertaining tourists and locals alike at festivals and parades. She has no problem talking about the supernatural and from all appearances has psychic sensitive abilities.

As we toasted completion of another parade appearance, I asked her if I could borrow her hearse for one of my book launches. She's the only one I know who would actually own a used hearse. She and her husband love Halloween and usually have a fake body in the back just for laughs.

The story she related happened a few years ago, on a Halloween night. The Ladies of the Evening Society always goes out in costume on Halloween, starting early at 3 or 4 p.m., to watch the hundreds of entertaining costumed kids mooching candy from willing shop owners. As things quiet down, we generally settle into drinks at Skylarks, watching for whatever ghosts might happen to be in there that night.

This particular Halloween, she was with a girlfriend, walking across the Fairhaven Village Green behind The Colophon Café and Village Books. A strange woman stood in the middle of the grassy square, dressed in what Lauren referred to as "old-time clothing. And not a wealthy woman, either." She was looking distressed and told the two she was looking for her husband.

"Maybe he's up there," joked Lauren, pointing to the dark, vacant, secret society 4th floor of the Pythias Building.

The woman looked up anxiously and was still staring upward as they walked off. It later occurred to Lauren that the woman was not in Halloween garb, was genuinely upset, and very likely not from the present. They had both seen her and spoken to her, but it began to dawn on her that the strange woman had been an apparition.

Fairhaven is famous for these types of stories. Pay attention to the clothing people wear. You may find that they bought their outfit in a store that closed 100 years ago.

Epilogue

Doing research for this book has changed me forever. I went into it expecting to write stories about "things that go bump in the night" and came out talking to the dead.

New technology, digital cameras and recorders now capture things only psychics could experience before. As I got deeper into the project, I began collecting "ghost hunting" equipment so I could investigate with the group from the Bellingham Observers of the Odd and Obscure (BOOO), instead of just observe them. The first time I got orb pictures, I was astounded and bought research books on the subject.

As I heard more and more digital recordings from things that weren't there, I began to understand that the departed seem to have gone to a parallel dimension and are generally eager to communicate. Unfortunately, we haven't a lot of control over their visitations to us. Their voices can be faint and their meaning obscure, orbs are challenged as dust spots, and they come and go as they please.

Once I understood that beings are visiting us continually, I was afraid at first. I can sometimes barely tolerate people in this world, let alone a whole bunch I can't see. I signed up for psychic courses and had conversations with extremely helpful local psychics like Sherry Mulholland and Jill Miller. They helped me understand that I had control over my personal boundaries and I was not at the mercy of any entity's whim.

If you grew up watching horror movies like the Exorcist, you may experience that fear, too. We like to worry about things we can't control. It's the stuff nightmares are made of. From my research in this small area of Historic Fairhaven, even "negative" entities don't have a lot of influence on us and can be handled by a visit from a professional.

Ghost Investigation type TV shows do a disservice to both psychics and spirits with participants harassing and challenging the dead to get reactions. It's just as rude as it would be if the person were alive. Poking at them and then running while screaming like a little girl is pointless and makes your EVPs useless. These shows sensationalize a serious subject. They also inspire people to try it themselves and can lead to disastrous encounters and spirits that won't leave.

My advice is to do your research, be polite, thank them when you leave, and ask them firmly not to come home with you. Don't taunt or tease a spirit that has been nice enough to make contact with you, and don't ever let teens use Ouija Boards or other such nonsense.

This is my first book on the spirits and it appears it won't be my last. Although my writings over the years have been almost exclusively business, marketing or "lifestyle" articles, I now add paranormal to that list. The allure of the unknown is addictive and there are many stories waiting to be told.

If you live in the Bellingham area and need help, please visit www.bellinghampsychics.com to find competent professionals in the business.

~Taimi

Resources

Print

- "Please the Customer First, The Brown & Cole Story," Ramon Heller, 1985

- "The Birth, Death and Resurrection of Fairhaven," George Hunsby, Chuckanut Editions, initially published 1975

- "Larrabee," C.X. Larrabee, 2nd, Published by Fairhaven Alumni Association, 2007

- "The Brothels of Bellingham," Curtis F. Smith, D.D.S., Whatcom County Historical Society, 2004

- "The Fairhaven Gazette," Tyrone and Penny Tillson, issues from 1980s to 1990s

- "Orbs, Their Mission and Messages of Hope," Klaus Heinemann, Ph.D. & Gundi Heinemann, Hay House, 2010

- "The Orb Project," Miceal Ledith, D.D., LLD, & Klaus Heinemann, Ph.D., Beyond Words Publishing, 2007

- "The Everything Ghost Hunting Book," Melissa Martin Ellis, Adams Media, 2009

- "The Everything Psychic Book," Michael R. Hathaway, DCH, Adams Media, 2011

- "Way Out Yonder," The Story of Fairhaven, William Lightfoot Visscher, 1898

◉ "Jim Wardner of Wardner, Idaho, By Himself," Jim Wardner, Anglo-American Publishing Co., 1900

◉ "Basic Psychic Development," John Friedlander & Gloria Hemsher, Weiser Books, 1999

◉ "How to Photograph the Paranormal," Leonore Sweet, Ph.D., Hampton Roads Publishing Co., 2005

Websites

◉ www.BellinghamBOOO.com   Bellingham Observers of the Odd and Obscure, Sherry Mulholland, webmaster

◉ www.mydarlinganna.com   Website based on the book, "My Darling Anna, The Life, Love & Legacy of W.R. Gray, Pioneer Physician" by Brian Griffin & Neelie Nelson

Acknowledgements

There are so many people who made this book possible by sharing their stories with me. Thank you all for contributing to this book and allowing your names to be used. These are not in any particular order. I apologize in advance if I missed anyone!   *~Taimi*

Psychics, Sensitives and Photographers
Sherry Mulholland, Psychic, Bellingham Observers of the Odd & Obscure
Pam Castanera, Psychic, Ghost Hunter
Brian Lee, Psychic, Ghost Hunter
Kandee Young, Sensitive
Leslie Smith, Photographer
Linda Sue Hoofnagle, Sensitive, Photographer
Penny Tillson, Fairhaven Historian, Energy Sensitive
Chuck Crooks, Psychic
Tracy Schwent, Sensitive
Joanna Schmidt, LMP, Intuitive
Elena Stecca, Psychic
Jill Miller, Psychic

Business Owners and Information Sources

April McAllister, Manager, Sycamore Square
Bill Lynch, Cheezeburger Signs
Brad & Jean Imus, Jacaranda Corp
Chuck Robinson, Village Books
David Killian, Colophon Café
Edward Davidson, former owner Wardner's Castle
Gordy Tweit, Fairhaven Pharmacy Museum
The Old Fairhaven Association
Ben Mann, Artist
Marijo Martini, Artist
Phyllis McKee, Finnegan's Alley
Anna Williams, Finnegan's Alley
Amy Electra Squires, Studio 910 Salon
Nancy Canyon, Artist
Don White, Skylark's
Donna Grasdock, Fairhaven Library
Cathy Lee, Southside Trends
Cassie Wolfkill, Southside Trends
Carla Lee, Whidbey Island Bank
Kelly Swordmaker, A Lot of Flowers
Penny Ferguson, A Lot of Flowers
Tina Schwindt, Bay to Baker Trading Co.
Steve Roguski, Fairhaven Runners
George Jartos, Artist/Cartoonist
Lillian Young, Mavis Gorman & Penny Tillson, editors

About the Author

Raised in Seattle, Taimi Dunn Gorman came to Bellingham to attend WWU and stayed. She has owned several businesses in Fairhaven including The Colophon Café, The Doggie Diner, and Gorman Publicity. As a freelance writer, she's published hundreds of lifestyle and business articles and photographs in dozens of magazines and newspapers, and is co-author of three Colophon Café cookbooks. She has taught Marketing and Public

Photo by Mark Turner.

Relations at Whatcom Community College and Western Washington University, and is a Marketing/PR consultant for numerous businesses. She lives in Bellingham with her husband, three dogs and a three-legged black cat.

In addition to writing, she now uses her newly discovered skill of spirit photography in local paranormal investigations.

A Note on the Type

The text of this book was set in Times New Roman, a serif typeface commissioned by the British newspaper *The Times* in 1931, created by Victor Lardent at the English branch of Monotype. The font was supervised by Stanley Morison and drawn by Victor Lardent, an artist from the advertising department of *The Times*. Morison used an older font named Plantin as the basis for his design, but made revisions for legibility and economy of space. The revision became known as Times New Roman and made its debut in the October 3rd, 1932 issue of *The Times* newspaper.

The book's title and chapter headings were set in Caslon Antique, a decorative American typeface that was designed in 1894 by Berne Nadall. It was originally called 'Fifteenth Century,' but was renamed Caslon Antique by Nadall's foundry, Barnhart Bros. & Spindler, in the mid-1920s. The design of the typeface is meant to evoke the Colonial era. Early printers would reuse metal type over and over again, and the faces would become chipped and damaged from use. Caslon Antique emulates this look.

Printed and bound on the Espresso Book Machine
Village Books, Bellingham, Washington
Designed by Kathleen Weisel